Endorsements

Adam Wittenberg has written a challenging message to his target audience. Drawing from his own journey, he provides heart searching questions for singles to ponder. I recommend *Single in Your 30s* as an inspirational study guide to help navigate your season of singleness.

> Mike Rizzo, Author of *Vertical Marriage: A Godward Preparation for Life Together*

***

It is refreshing to read a book that is birthed out of real life experience with the gift of God our Father's perspective.

I recommend this book because I know the heart and reach of Adam. He has been an inspiration and friend for years here at IHOPKC with a steadfast walk both as a single man and now as a married man with a wife who is a gift from heaven!

What a challenging hour we live relationally in this culture and nation. We often spend much of our time pressing our opinions into how we live life, hoping it is connected to lasting Truth.

I believe Adam gives some great advice that is peppered with God's perspective that can help the person reaching for a commitment in marriage to raise a higher standard and be confident in the journey they are on.

Thank you Adam for your insightful, honest words that you have penned for us to strengthen our relationships and answer an often challenging path of what it is to travel in life to a Godly, fulfilling marriage!

Craig Steinle, Dean of Men, International House of Prayer University, Grandview, Missouri

***

My wife and I celebrated 20 years of marriage last year, and I can honestly say it is now Heaven on Earth! However, being married at 19 and 20, I wish we would have had this book in our hands then. I know the title is *Single in Your 30's*, but Adam's wisdom and vulnerability would have helped me so tremendously as a teenager who was engaged in high school. Even as my wife and I are now in our 40's, the insight we have gleaned in reading through Adam's journey is *still* helpful.

In this book, there is much practical relational insight that transcends age and marital status. After having been through seasons of a broken marriage, mistrust, physical separation, and emotional disconnection, I can honestly say that the seeds sown in this book will help any single - or newly-wed - reading this book find a place of health and deep intimacy that we all crave. Whatever is not crucified and healed *before* marriage will be crucified and healed *through* the journey of marriage—and that may be more painful than you think! Therefore, beloved, take heed to the spirit of this work!

David Lee Brown, Pastor of SA Tabernacle House of Prayer, and Author of *Hearing Love: A life Application Commentary on the Greatest Commandment*

***

I had the privilege of knowing Adam before he met his wife while he was single in his 30s, and this is a man who I would want to have had some advice from back when I was in my own single journey.

Adam is practical, down to earth, and he loves the Lord.

If you are single and in your 30s, or if you have a passion for connecting singles, this book is definitely worth trying!

Courtney M., Kansas City, Missouri

SINGLE IN YOUR 30'S

SINGLE IN YOUR 30'S

How to Know if You're Avoiding Marriage & What to Do About It

by

Adam Wittenberg

Copyright

"Then the LORD God said, 'It is not good for the man to be alone. I will make a helper who is just right for him.'"

Genesis 2:18, NLT

"Two are better than one..."

Ecclesiastes 4:9

Dedication

I want to dedicate this book to my Lord and Savior, Jesus Christ, who I believe inspired it; to my beautiful wife, Stephany, who is God's greatest human gift to me; and to the singles at IHOPKC who have been with me on this journey and helped inspire this book. I'm pulling for you, I care deeply about you, and I want to see each of you achieve your full destiny in God, including godly marriage.

Thanks to everyone who helped with this book, from those who read to those who edited, encouraged, or helped with layout and design. It truly takes a team!

Adam Wittenberg

March 2023

#SingleInYour30sBook

TABLE OF CONTENTS

TABLE OF CONTENTS

Introduction:

A PROPHETIC CALL FOR SINGLES TO FIND LOVE, MARRIAGE, AND RELATIONSHIPS

Let's face it, marriage is the norm for the vast majority of people. It always has been and—I pray—always will be. Just because society and the church have changed their views doesn't mean that God has. And I believe God will give this gift to the vast majority of people who believe Him for it. God is not subject to societal limitations. He can make rivers in the desert and he does the impossible every day. But the devil's plan has been to overwhelm people in fear and doubt to get us to forfeit our God-given rights and blessings. I don't want marriage to become a god or an idol to you, but I'm trying to reassure you that the desire, hunger, and yearning to be married is real, is good and is from God.

This is where so many Christians get hung up: They think that they're weird for desiring marriage, that they should be tougher. They say, "I'll be able to be single." Now I'm all for grace to have seasons of singleness and I've had a few myself, but I think we've taken a good thing (marriage) and turned it into something bad. That's what this book is looking to correct. We've created a false normalcy about being single when really many of us are scared—of God, ourselves, and others. We've developed a whole list of excuses about why we're single, when often we're afraid to face that we're bitter, disappointed, and not trusting God's love and plan for us.

It doesn't matter how you got here—you may find yourself single because your relationships didn't work out, or maybe you tried marriage and it ended in a divorce, or you're still waiting for 'the one.' Whatever your circumstances are, your dreams and desires are not forfeited because of sin. Just like when we get saved, it requires sincere repentance and turning to Christ so He can make something new out of our lives.

Whatever your experiences, I want to encourage you to turn from the past and ask the Lord for a fresh perspective. Most of us have built up walls that the Lord wants to take down. There will be times I encourage you to examine the past to remove hurt or bitterness, especially if there are vows or things you've said about what will or won't happen in the future because of your past sin. ('I'll never get married,' 'No one will ever want me,' etc.). Definitely delete that and some of your old perspectives which may be preventing you from getting happily married.

It doesn't matter if you're a virgin, if you're tall or short, rich or poor, dark or light, shy or outgoing. Marriage is the norm for almost all of us, and you don't have to repent for desiring it. We may need to change some of our attitudes, actions and beliefs, but the desire itself is good.

Let's journey together toward hope and wholeness. I assure you God wants to give it to you!

Chapter 1

WHAT I SEE:
THE STATE OF SINGLENESS

Singleness is at an all-time high (a recent survey found that nearly half of American adults are single, or about 128 million people!) This comes from a decade's-long trend that was only worsened by the coronavirus events of 2020 and beyond. As more people 'go it alone,' society has become more isolated and fragmented. It's harder to connect and harder to get married. Don't think the devil doesn't want it this way—he knows that isolated people are easier to pick off—but God still has a plan. (I take comfort in Malachi 4:5-6, which talks of the restoration of families before the Lord's return.)

Add to this the decades-long trend of delaying marriage in the name of education, career and personal pursuits. This has some benefits, as marrying a bit later can lead to more stability. And certainly for a lot of women, the training or advanced training they've received has enabled them to achieve success that would not have been possible without higher levels of education or investment in their careers. I'm not going to address what to do about those issues as that is not the focus of this book. Only you and God know how to navigate education, career and the like. What I am here to help navigate is our attitudes about relationships. Let's take a look at how we prioritize, hide from, or dismiss our desire for marriage, and our pursuit (or lack of pursuit) of that relationship!

If you're a woman you may be thinking, "But I'm not supposed to pursue relationships, that's the man's job!" And while you are ultimately right, a godly woman can do a lot to encourage or show an openness to, or perhaps in some rightful ways pursue, a relationship without trying to take over the man's role. There are better resources about this topic (*Wild at Heart* by John Eldredge comes to mind, a book not only for men but insightful for women as well, or its counterpart, *Captivating*). What's more important than role, however, is the attitude, motive and belief (or unbelief) that guides your actions. Scripture says that "Man looks at the outward appearance, but God looks at the heart" (1 Samuel 16:7).

This book is written from a Christian perspective, rooted in what the Bible says about forgiveness, repentance and the new life that is available in Jesus Christ. If you don't know Him and what He's done for you, I urge you to read the Gospel of Mark and Gospel of John, biographies of Jesus found in the Bible, and to talk to a friend or family member that has a strong faith. You can also talk to the Lord directly —He will hear you when you call! Tell Him you want to know Him and come into that saving relationship. He loves to respond!

This is ultimately a helpful book. I'm writing it because I believe you want to break free of or become aware of false beliefs about love, dating, relationships, and marriage; that you want change, and that you want a different result than what you've seen before. There is a better way!

One definition of insanity is doing the same thing over and over again and expecting a different result. I did this for much of my thirties, and ended the decade single. It wasn't until I came to the end of myself that God was able to move in, bring my marriage partner, and set me on a new course. He truly did lift me out of the pit and set me on a high place. I want the same for you! This was not my own doing; my role was to cooperate, humble myself, and fall at His feet. Then came a time when I needed to spring up and take action; the rest, as they say, is history.

Set a Vision

As you approach this book, I encourage you to set a fresh vision. The vision could be about where you want to go or the type of marriage you desire. It could be about reclaiming your past vision of being happily married or finding your spouse. Even if it seems out of reach, begin to think on this vision.

Then ask yourself, "Is marriage really better than singleness?" Because if it is, then it's worth laying hold of, no matter the cost. If you don't want to spend the next decade single (I'm assuming you're already in your thirties, or beyond), then let's start laying out a vision of what we want in marriage, believe that it's worth pursuing, and start a course to pursue it. And that course will likely start with you—not with circumstance and not with another person but with what *you* think and believe, because I find those are often the biggest barriers.

It's time to stop making excuses, blaming others, or hiding behind religious baggage. **The reason why most of us that aren't married in our thirties is because we don't want to be, because we harbor guilt or shame, don't like or trust ourselves, or are mad at God, our parents, or the world**. None of this is good soil for the Kingdom of God (see Mark 4:3-9), so the process usually starts with taking a garden hoe to our hearts. That is where we will begin.

Chapter 2

My Story & Call

My thirties were full of extremes: trying not to date, hiding and telling myself that I was OK being single, then rushing into dating the moment a good opportunity came along (and quickly making a mess of things!). From running and hiding to hot pursuit—and I could change in a moment. It felt as if my words were worthless —because they were: a feigned attempt to hide my insecurities and fears behind a bunch of religious language. All to try to conceal that I was a lonely, self-loathing, and depressed soul, dealing with a boatload of issues around love, sex, and relationships.

This book is an attempt to spare others from a similar journey. Hopefully you will see yourself in these pages and escape from the patterns that consumed over a decade of my life until God had mercy and brought me the woman who is now my wife. But it took getting to the end of myself, and getting over myself, for this to happen. "When the power of the holy people is completely shattered ..." is when God breaks in (Daniel 12:7).

If you are a single man, you will hear a prophetic call to godly action. This includes recognizing where you may be off, identifying lies you may have embraced, and finding steps to confession and repentance. I'm not saying that everyone single in their thirties is ungodly or in error. I actually do know people, and have experienced a few periods of grace myself, where I knew that it was God's will for me to be without a mate for a while.

Just to prove the point, I met a man on the West coast who spent about a decade ministering in Los Angeles. He seemed like a perfectly normal guy who was doing the Lord's work. There didn't appear to be anything wrong with him or anything he was hiding; he was just committed to doing the work and had grace to do it. I'm sure there were moments of loneliness or struggles, but he had a sobriety about him and a calmness in his spirit. He presented himself straight up and told his story without fanfare. There was no alter-agenda.

After about a decade of faithful service, when he was in his mid-thirties, he met a beautiful young woman. They got married and quickly started a family. The transition wasn't jarring for him. He had served the Lord faithfully as a single man, and now God blessed him with a mate. He didn't have to present a bunch of lies or justifications when he was single for why he wasn't married; he just knew it wasn't the time or the Lord hadn't brought his wife into the picture. There was nothing he was hiding or running from, or anything blocking him from getting married other than the season he was in—which also meant that he had grace to remain single for that season. He entered marriage cleanly. That is not the case with most singles I encounter.

What struck me about this guy was his sense of personal responsibility. Real men (and women) take ownership of their lives. If they're single, it's because they want to be in that season and they are truly content waiting on God. This guy walked in that grace, never giving up on or denying that he wanted marriage, and in due time he reaped his reward. He resisted bitterness, blaming, or excuses. God responds to faith.

This type of behavior is sadly more common in the world. The world (or secular, non-Christian people) won't put up with these excuses. There's no one else to blame but you if you're single and not pursuing relationships (especially for men). You're not waiting on anything except your own desires, or lack thereof. The ball's in your court, and your friends would look at you funny if you said half the stuff that Christian guys do about why they're not married (or even dating). Perhaps we need this very sober reality check!

If you can't take responsibility now for where you are, how will you do it when the right woman and circumstance comes along? If you're incompetent and a victim, how about when you have real responsibilities? This does not bode well or make you more attractive, or suited, for marriage. Many a woman has had to pick up the reigns and coax the guy to step up. I'm OK with that to a limited extent—a woman can help awaken a man, but she cannot make him one. Either he rises into his destiny or remains forever a boy, needy for the next prompt or tug to get him to do what he is designed to do. God has a better way.

I think one of the healthy ways I've seen it said is, "This just isn't a focus for me right now." I think that's one of the main differences between people who truly have a gift of singleness, especially for a season, and those who are faking it or pretending that they do. The single-minded person can say, "This isn't my focus" or, "This isn't the time for that; I have other things that I'm doing and I'm at peace with it." The faker is saying words to that effect but has absolutely no peace. They are either on the edge of their seat looking for their mate, or beating themselves up daily and trying to solve a problem that they can't bear to face openly (i.e., admit to others).

LOOK BENEATH THE SURFACE.
LOOK WITHIN.

I'm always looking for underlying issues, for places where the walk doesn't match the talk, because that was my case for years. I claimed to be OK being single; I claimed that this was good, and everything was OK for me, but most of that time I was feeling doubt, fear, or desire for marriage and yet I was hiding, suppressing, and denying it. That's the point of this book—to come out of denial—and I'm not afraid to use some pointed words to get you there.

So, again, if you're a man, be prepared to be called out. Be prepared to ask yourself some tough questions, to hear some tough things and attempt to have a more honest dialogue. If some of these things apply to you, begin to wrestle with it and take corrective action. If they don't, you can move on, but know that you probably know or will come across people that are in some of these predicaments and I want to equip you to minister to them.

If you're a single woman reading this book, I will also offer plenty of advice, hard questions, and things to ask yourself on your journey. This comes from years of observing single friends who also have given all kinds of reasons and excuses for being single. A lot of the questions I'm going to ask are about your attitude and thought process. Do you really want marriage? Do you really want a man and all that it means to be with one? Are you over yourself? Do you believe deep inside that you're worthy and suited for marriage? These are important questions.

Sadly, a whole ethos has emerged in society that it's better to be single, that the happiest people are single and that real freedom comes from being single. Not just men, but many women have bought into this lie and are even seduced by it. I'll talk about female empowerment and what I believe are the right, and wrong, ways to go about that, including ways that don't put off marriage or disparage it. We must recognize that marriage has been under a terrible attack for decades and the endemic of singleness is an outgrowth of what society has tried to do to marriage in general.

Many women, including Christians, have been caught up in these lies, not because they want to but simply because the culture has repeated it so many times. I have a lot of compassion for you. I want to see you and all my single friends who desire marriage, which is the vast majority, happily married and ending their season of singleness. That is my intent in this book.

This may also be a useful resource for families and friends of singles in their thirties. With these tools, you can spot some of the lies and falsehoods that people in my generation have bought into. No, I don't just go around telling people that they've done this or that and accusing them of believing lies. It's always best to inquire; like I've said, the gentleman above had real grace to be single for about a decade. And I, too, have had short seasons where I knew it wasn't God's will for me to date or pursue a relationship. It's not one-size-fits-all, but I believe this book will allow you to see through many things that older singles hide behind when they truly need to get over their issues and move toward a relationship.

So, again, I urge you to read this with an open heart, a willingness to reflect and ask yourself hard questions, and a willingness to challenge some of your normal assumptions about love, marriage, and relationships.

Are you ready for a fresh take?

THE MAIN POINT

The main point of this book is to get over yourself and the ungodly attitudes and beliefs you may have bought into. They are all around us. I'm not saying they're all your fault, but you are ultimately the only one that can change you. Change starts with your mindset, like the apostle Paul says, "to be transformed by the renewing of your mind" (Romans 12:2). This is ultimately a mind-renewal book. My goal is for you to be able to spot lies in yourself and others, and to get delivered so you can deliver others. And yes, of course, to get married and form happy family relationships. Be blessed, reader, and know that I'm with you in the fight!

SINGLE IN YOUR 30'S

Remember …

It's about seasons not lies …
Bitterness can hold you back …
Breakthrough starts within!

Chapter 3

FACING OUR PASTS

My Past...I grew up in a home where marriage was not a good thing. My parents had a bad relationship that many years later ended in divorce. They did not present a good picture of marriage, and I was hesitant to desire it because it didn't seem to work for either of them. The pain and trauma that I witnessed was enough to make me doubt the institution of marriage, as well as myself in all kinds of ways.

Would I fall into these same sinful patterns?
Would I do it better or have the same faults?
Could I even trust myself?

I won't wax long on that, at least not right here, but those seeds of doubt about marriage and about myself plagued me throughout my twenties, thirties, and even my very early forties. It's these things that I saw in myself, and often see in others, that I mostly want to address. It's often hard to spot, but I can almost assure you some of these same things could be in you.

You may be thinking, "But Adam, I didn't grow up in a dysfunctional family. My parents loved each other and had a great marriage. How could this book apply to me?" Sometimes, the wounding comes later in life. It could be resentment over friends who've gotten married, or not getting picked by someone that you liked, or just bad messages from the culture. Sometimes bad messages tear you down. Messages like, "You're not good enough" or, "You're not doing the right things to get a spouse" or, "You're not worthy."

Or, there's the other side of pride and puffiness that I've seen people develop, an insular nature of "I don't need anyone" or, "I'm good on my own, leave me alone"; "No one's worthy of me." I've seen this in both men and women.

Let's face it: the dating world is hard! Even the phenomenon of modern dating is not friendly ground. Do you realize that for most of human history people did not date in the way they do today? This is a very modern construct, where most of the family members are removed and even much of society. It's left almost entirely to the individuals to determine if they like each other, if they're a good fit, etc.

Again, this is very abnormal in most of the world, although it is becoming increasingly common as the secular West spreads its culture globally. However, back to my point. The world is harsh and the dating world too, and the walls we build to protect ourselves are often what is keeping us from experiencing ultimate breakthrough. So even if you grew up in a more stable and loving home, there may be attitudes, lies, or behaviors you've developed that keep you from finding what you really want.

And then there's one more focus here, which is the Christian world and all the psychobabble and even misuse of Scripture and spiritual principles to mask our desires or disappointments, or to hide and perpetuate singleness, when that's not most people's true calling. If you've ever read *Wild at Heart* by John Eldredge (which I highly recommend, for both men and women), he says singleness is a real but very rare gift, and something like one in 1,000 men have it. He fundamentally calls men into action and to pursue authentic lives, which include a battle to fight, a beauty to rescue, and an adventure to live. This is what we are made for.

I want to do the same, calling both sexes to be authentic in their pursuit and their emotions, actions, words, and beliefs.

MAD AT GOD!

One of the ways I've grown since my childhood is in how I deal with my anger toward God. We've all done that before, though, right? We've projected our anger over not getting what we want at Him. I've done this many times, and you can even see examples of this behavior in biblical figures like King David in the Psalms. I spent a lot of my singleness angry at God for not giving me what I thought I deserved.

When something doesn't go the way we want it to, we often create a new path or plan that suits our dysfunction, put a Christian label on it, and say, "This is the way, I'm going to walk in it." It could go something like this:

"God, you haven't given me a spouse even though I've been faithful to you. I'm mad or feel like a failure in this area, but I know I can't turn from you. So here's my plan: I'm going to hide myself in the church, in hard work, in serving, or in any number of other things. Good things (I know better than to run to blatant sin), but I'm truly mad at you. I'm hiding, fearful, and insecure. I'm disappointed in you, in men, in women, in my family, in the lot I've been dealt in life. But again, I'm here for you, God. And here's where I'm going to stay, trapped in my own little box or my own little world, doing the things I feel safe doing, in your name, until either you leave me here or send someone or something to break me out. PS—I love you."

It's almost like we're daring God to come get us! We're actually testing if He really loves us and will give us the promised things and make it happen the way that we've wanted. Who's kingdom are we seeking? His or ours? It's worth asking. Now, again, I'd rather have people running to the Lord, even in these broken forms, than running into blatant sin. Yes, of course, but this is where you don't get a free pass from me. And whether you see this in yourself or in people that you know, this is often what I've found with people in their thirties who are still single in the church.

I can't entirely blame you, because it's better to turn to the Lord than to the world, but the Lord is after the hurt in our heart, the bitterness, the resentment and pain. He is the healer, and He has glorious solutions. Again, as I'll talk about in the book, it's often worldly people who don't have the same hang-ups because they don't have a God to blame it on. They simply take responsibility for themselves and, if they're mad they say it. If they want something, they go for it, and if they want a change, they make it.

I remember once a pastor asking me if I was truly happy. I remember giving some kind of religious answer, "Oh, yes, of course," or something, but he was right. He didn't press the issue in the moment, but it did plant that seed of doubt or a reflection point of, "No, I'm not happy. I'm not fulfilled. I'm not completely content in my singleness." Ask yourself the same questions: Are you truly happy? Is this all there is? Or would you, if the right person or situation came along, immediately begin to pursue that relationship or be excited that someone was pursuing you? If you answer 'yes' to the second question, then keep reading.

The Day of Reckoning

Now that I've told you my story, let's think about yours. When you turned thirty, how did you react? With disappointment? Or with discouragement?

If you were that disappointed about not being married, how will you handle disappointment when you are married?

If you're just a disappointed and victimized person, then you're not well-suited for marriage. Not yet, anyway. First, you need to repent. Then, you will need to grow and seek God in order to heal those broken places in your character.

LIVING A FALSE NORMAL

I believe many of us—maybe even you—are living in a false normal. Because the longer you do something, the more you think it's normal. The longer you've been single, the more it becomes easier to tell yourself that this is what life is. But it's not normal or the fullness of life for the vast majority of us. You have to break this mindset and begin to examine the reasons you're single. Is it fear of commitment? Fear of being hurt? Fears and reservations about the opposite-sex or about marriage itself? Fear of loss of independence? It could also be rampant insecurity or instability in your life, or just lies you've bought into from the culture, and sadly the church, about what is normal or expected.

If we don't admit there's a problem, there's nothing to solve or change. You've probably heard the quote that one definition of insanity is doing the same thing over and expecting different results. It might be time to ask yourself some hard questions about your expectations and behaviors.

Let me be clear: I'm not saying it's necessarily your fault that you're single at thirty. I'm not guaranteeing that something's wrong. But we live in a broken and increasingly ungodly world, and if one of the devil's greatest fears is the Bride of Christ arising and a Jesus generation that will walk like Him, do the greater works and prepare the earth for His return, then it makes sense why marriage and children are under such attack.

If the devil can't keep you from marriage, then at least he hopes to delay it and minimize the number of children you'll have. I believe that's his ultimate goal, besides human misery and suffering. It's proven that married people are on average happier, have the best sex lives, live longer, and a host of other benefits. Of course the devil would want to deny you those blessings, as well as cut off godly offspring (see Malachi 2:15).

Even the divorce rate (which is *not* 50 percent like they tell you, not even close—see Appendix A) is an attempt to sabotage marriage and normalize divorce. The devil must be really threatened! He is the father of lies after all.

The longer you're single, the easier it is to make up stories about why rather than to face the facts. The story is almost never what it seems or what's really holding us back. And the longer you wait, the more unrealistic your expectations can become about marriage, sex, and what your spouse will be like. It takes rigorous discipline to avoid fantasy and delusion, and it's often a process to come out of it. God didn't make us to go it alone (Genesis 2:18). Start your journey of repentance today!

GAMES (SINGLE) PEOPLE PLAY

Before we close this chapter of reflection on our stories and past behaviors, I want to take a look at the games single people play because I played most or all of them. Really, it's a form of mental gymnastics, hiding, denying, and pretending; anything to prevent yourself or others from seeing your disappointment and pain. These "games" include anything from telling yourself you're OK, that you don't really want marriage, that it's not that important to you (when it really is), that you're not jealous of your friends that have gotten married (but you are), that you're not secretly seething whenever you hear about another couple getting married (this is a big one).

There's also cutting corners and doing things like engaging in premarital sex. Whether in a 'committed' relationship or through causal encounters, this is *NOT* God's way for us to live. We must quit all forms of unrighteousness and cling to His plan. He forgives and wants to give us the best things, but we've got to turn.

The offended heart is a seedbed for all kinds of dysfunction. It clouds your vision and prevents you from seeing others, and yourself (and sometimes God) clearly. This must be cleared up, and the games—lies—eliminated. Things WILL get easier if you do this. Even if it means you'll have to face some painful things (I certainly did, like my years of self-loathing and shame), at least you'll be battling against the real enemy and making progress, not fighting imaginary battles that are fruitless. "I don't fight as one who beats the air …" Paul wrote in 1 Corinthians 9:26, but instead he called us to "fight the good fight." You can't do this until you admit what the enemy is, and very often the enemy lies within.

It's time to ask yourself some hard questions. Note your answers. Don't couch them in religious language, but answer honestly. Sometimes you may want to pretend you're not a Christian and just say what you honestly think. What is the first thing that pops in your head? Not something you overthink, but what comes from your heart. This alone can bring a great breakthrough of honesty.

The truth is we all have a past. We all have bad behaviors. But we also have the Bible as our guidepost and a loving and forgiving heavenly Father who wants more for us. Admitting our wounds, shortcomings, and sin can only improve our lives, single or not.

Chapter 4

DATING FALLACIES

The Friend Zone…One of the worst things I've seen singles in their thirties do is remain in the friend zone. Yes, this can be a problem for younger singles, but I particularly want to call out older, mature singles who should know what they're looking for and should be out pursuing marriage, not casual relationships (even if it is just friends). I remember talking to a guy who was about to turn forty. He said he had just broken up with a girl he had been dating for THREE YEARS! Now I'm assuming she wasn't eighteen, but was at least similar in age or out of her mid-to-late twenties.

You should know yourself by that point in life and have a good grasp on who you are, what you're looking for and what you want out of life. Even if the other person is younger, if you're the older one in the relationship, you should be looking out for those things. I find it almost inexcusable that a man of that age would need THREE YEARS to date and figure out if he wanted to get married! There may have been extenuating circumstances and every situation is different, but please, friends, this is NOT the norm!

BOY MEETS GIRL

When I met my wife, I was 41 and she was 32. I was attracted to her immediately and slowly began to build a friendship with her, getting to know her in group settings. I wasn't ready for pursuit because I was in a season of intense inner healing, and I knew this, but she was on my radar from the start. I gave off no mixed signals and did not "awaken love before it's time" (Song 2:7), because I wasn't ready to do anything about the feelings that I had. I also hadn't tested them to know if they were real or just fascination.

About six months into knowing her, the Lord began to touch and complete the season of healing I was in. I immediately began to feel better, and within two weeks, connected with Stephany in a special way and began to pursue her. We started talking engagement after two months, and were married less than five months from the time I began pursuing her. There was no awkward middle phase. Once I decided I liked her and wanted to pursue her, I moved forward.

She was receptive, and we put marriage on the table pretty early. As we moved closer to getting engaged, we checked with our spiritual advisors to talk through any red flags or roadblocks and, upon finding none, proceeded with the engagement. We also signed up for premarital counseling, which I always recommend, as we did not want to enter marriage blindly. All told, we went from met to married in eleven months: six months as acquaintances and casual friends; two and-a-half months of pursuit and dating; and two and-a-half months from engagement to marriage.

I was on a marriage track, and both of us knew that we weren't looking to date casually. We also knew that the other person didn't have to be "perfect," but a great match, highly compatible in most regards. We'd each been through enough junk in our own lives, and dating lives, to spot the fake and know that we didn't want to mess around, play with hearts, or lead the other person on. We were safe to move forward and did so with ease and confidence, even as we planned our wedding in 70 days. It was a beautiful day, surrounded by God's joy and grace.

BENEFITS OF FASTING

If you are in your thirties and have a large number of opposite gender friends, or even if you have just one or two that are very significant to you (especially if your "best friend" is opposite gender), it may be time to ask yourself some hard questions: Am I truly friends with this person or just using them to soothe the loneliness? I was super intentional during my thirties about relationships with the opposite sex. I didn't do a lot of random hangouts with girls or one-on-

ones. I tried very carefully to avoid one-on-ones with women that I wasn't pursuing or interested in pursuing. Unless there was a specific reason to be alone with them, I made a strong effort not to do so. This was to guard my heart as well as theirs, to not send mixed signals and to avoid stirring up (or awakening) love before it's time.

I think many of us may need to fast from some of our opposite sex relationships for a time if we're not interested in pursuing them for marriage, but truly desire marriage. Sometimes good really is the enemy of best. Now I know sometimes you meet your spouse through one of your friends so I'm not telling you what to do, but I am urging you to examine your motives, pray about it, and to see if there could be some benefit to abstaining from the fulfillment you're getting from this person so that you can seek fulfillment in the person who is going to become your spouse.

Harsh words, I know, but if marriage is what you want then make sure you're making time and space to pursue it, not filling it with halfway substitutes (this includes all forms of casual sex, casual dating, and other unproductive relationships). You won't regret less "friend" time with an opposite gender friend but you *will* regret delaying meeting your spouse because you filled that time and space with other things.

What Are Your Expectations?

Now that we're talking about finding a mate, it's fair to ask, "What are your expectations?" Will prince charming come up on a white horse, sweep you off your feet, and carry you into your "Happily ever after?" For guys, will a supermodel emerge from the water, lock eyes with you, walk in your direction, smile and hold you in a never-ending embrace? More importantly, are you looking for that "perfect" man or "perfect" woman, someone with no defects, hurts, or hang-ups? Someone who's just like you only opposite gender? Someone who compliments you perfectly, never disappoints you or makes you mad, has no more growing up to do but is perfect in every way?

Now, I'm not a fan of marrying someone who is immature and hasn't dealt with their issues. This is a red flag. But expecting someone to be perfect and need no more growth is delusional and even destructive.

Sadly, I've seen many women, and sometimes men, take out their frustration on the opposite sex by declaring "all men are scum," disparaging the opposite gender, and setting an impossible standard for their future spouse to meet because they are so afraid of getting hurt. To respond to this, I want to tell my wife's story.

By her early thirties, my wife had been through enough of life and relationships to know that men aren't perfect. She also knew, however, that it was better for her to go through life with a man than without one. Despite her ups and downs and disappointments with men, she never gave up on the idea of marriage. She never turned her heart and concluded she would be better off without one or that men were unworthy. She continued to desire what was natural: to be wed, have a husband, and to build a happy life.

I think many young women in our culture would be well-served by her example, because if you have unrealistic expectations of men, of marriage, or of life in general, you are sure to be disappointed. If you bought into the fairytale or myth, you will see things come crashing down quickly when you encounter real life. This is part of the Hollywood sensation that has messed with the minds of many a young person, and older people as well. You don't need half the things you think you need, and half the things you try won't make you happy (probably more than half if we take the eternal wisdom in the Bible about the vanities of life).

Let's spare ourselves a boatload of heartache and stick with the timeless wisdom, that the best things in life are to love and serve God, work hard, and keep His commandments. God designed it in the beginning for a man and a woman to be together in marriage and that is still His plan for the vast majority of humanity. It doesn't matter how advanced we are, how much our culture has lied to us and told us that we've changed or that it's changed. Human nature *hasn't* changed.

The book of Ecclesiastes tells us that nothing is new under the sun. Let's start living like it. Let's start aligning our thoughts, will, and emotions toward the truth. The sooner we come to these realizations and stop blaming our circumstances or others, the sooner we can pray in alignment with God's will and see His kingdom come and will be done, on earth as it is in heaven. Let's get out of fantasy, the blame game, and any other number of excuses that we make and start aligning with the will of God. All of heaven is waiting.

Many Christian singles think they're being judged by God, that there's something wrong with them or that they've sinned and that's why they're still single. That their being single is a mark of judgment from God. And sometimes they're right! What strikes me about worldly people (non-Christians) is they could've had multiple unrighteous relationships and yet they're still hoping, believing and wanting to get married. They don't count their past sins against them because they don't believe that they have sinned or know that they have. This lack of guilt, and, therefore, lack of doubt, leads them to keep moving forward.

My heart is not to endorse sin, not at all, but for Christians to access the very real forgiveness of

God and walk in the truth that, "there's therefore now no condemnation for those who are in Christ Jesus" (Romans 8:1). Regretting your sins and learning from them is good and godly behavior, but don't allow them to define your worth and determine your future. This is where looking at worldly people, even for a moment, and then looking at the truth of Scripture, which is supreme, can help us. Maybe that's why I'm bringing up the world: as a challenge to religious Christians who think they're doing everything right but don't have the fruit of righteousness or the reward they are seeking and are mad or frustrated.

What We Can Learn From Worldly Women (and Men)

Worldly women are more assertive. They want something and they go after it. While I'm not a fan of everything secular women do to find a guy (such as casual and premarital sex), we can glean some things from their experience. For starters, they take responsibility for their singleness, instead of putting it all on God or others. There are often two extremes: 1. That it's all on God, or 2. That it's all on us. So, what is reality? Partnership. Participation by both parties. This is what God's after.

Now there's a right and a wrong way to do this. Abraham "helping God" by sleeping with Hagar was not God's plan to bring forth offspring. But Abraham did have to keep pursuing his wife, Sarah, even though she was well passed her childbearing years (God had promised them a son in their old age).

At least secular women are working on it. At least they're pursuing something (or allowing themselves to be pursued). It's like the buffet card at Brazilian barbecue. Is your card red or green? What vibe are you giving off? There could be a relationship right in front of you. Are you open to it? Or do you have to be Lord of your own life?

Real women carry themselves with identity, a quiet, subtle confidence (which is very sexy). They portray strength and yet an openness to being pursued. It's going to be work because they don't want just any old guy, but it can be done. This is not about a certain personality type, but about inward conviction and identity.

Some Other Things We Can Learn From Worldly People

Worldly people do not beat themselves up like Christians do. They don't tend to focus on their faults. Maybe it's because they haven't repented of their sins so they're not even conscious that they have sinned or are a sinner. Whatever the reason, they tend to be freer in pursuing what they want and going after it.

Christians, on the other hand, tend to be way too conscious of sin, sometimes taking that on as an identity. It's just one more way that we hide and declare ourselves unworthy. The funny thing is, yes, we have sinned and come short of God's perfect standard, but if we confess our sins, He is faithful and just to forgive us and cleanse us of all unrighteousness (1 John 1:8-9). Therefore, sin is no longer our identity and we're not subject to its penalty.

I could write a whole sermon on this right now, but my point is simply that we're not glorifying God when we remain continually focused on our sin and what terrible people we are, especially if we have repented of it and asked Jesus to forgive us. We glorify Him by walking in the newness of life that He died and rose to give. And this new life includes freedom and confidence—things I see more often in worldly people who have no concept of sin.

Again, I don't approve of sin and I'm not soft on it (I actually do a lot of evangelism trying to call lost people to repentance). They are condemned and on their way to hell without Christ. But Jesus said the people of this age are savvier in dealing with their own kind than the people of faith and urged us to learn some things from them (see Luke 16:8). Perhaps this could be one of them! (Side note—there are plenty of scriptures that urge us to walk free of guilt, shame, and condemnation, so this is very biblical, but for some reason many of us need an in-person example or to get provoked by the actions of worldly people. I'm not sure why that is.)

Interactions in the world tend to be clearer. You dance with a girl and you both have a role to play in seeing if it goes further. I feel like much in Christian dating is so multi-layered before even getting to the point of a coffee date, dancing (if you believe in that) or even interacting with someone you'd like to pursue. What's helpful is to find someone who's not intimidated by members of the opposite sex and exudes confidence (or openness, not anger or resentment), then pray and act. Keep praying and acting and see where things go.

I remember a season when I went on several dates with girls I met online, and then dated a girl I met in person. This served two things: to get me back in the dating field (which some worldly friends urged me to do), and also taught me how to end, or have a relationship ended. None of these got super serious. No one was leading the other person on or playing with hearts. It was taking a chance, going on a few dates and deciding if I wanted to continue (or sometimes the other person decided). This was a healthy reality check from the Christian fantasy that I was only going to date one person and then marry them. This can and does happen, but it's not as common as it should be, and, if you've made it to your thirties and aren't married, chances are it's not the plan for you!

I certainly think it's good to date for marriage, particularly if you are mid-to-late twenties or in your thirties, but it doesn't prevent you from going on a few dates to get to know someone and then decide if you want to pursue them more seriously. As long as that's clear from the start, there is no harm or foul.

Now mind you, these were women I met online or one that I met at church through a friend. I didn't really know any of them. This is what allowed me to date them as friends to get more acquainted to decide if I (or they) wanted to go further. This would not be the same with someone I knew, was attracted to and wanted to pursue but was afraid. This is where many people, especially guys, keep girls in limbo by making it seem like they want to hang out as friends because they are scared to make their intentions known. The woman ends up frustrated because the guy plays on their emotions but won't get serious. Don't do this! We've got to love one another better than that!

Worldly men (and women) are upfront about what they want. If they want to get married, they say so. If they don't want to get married, they say so. There's not much of a middle and there's none of the hemming and hawing, while Christians put up a front and say, "I want to get married, but I'm OK being single," "I don't know if I want to get married," or, "I'll just be single until the rapture," to camouflage their pain, fear, and disappointment with God about their current situation. Wouldn't it be more productive to simply be honest about our feelings and needs?

Chapter 5

Lies That Are Keeping You From Marriage

Many of us are believing lies that are keeping us from getting married. My question to those of us engaged in this behavior is: What are you overcompensating for, hiding behind, or obfuscating?

I'd say to you: Quit trying to fast away all of your desires such that you have none remaining. That's not even biblical—it's more like Buddhism! Stop trying to become so humble that nothing affects you, that you have nothing else to hope for or pursue. That's also not biblical.

Why are we making things so hard? What are we running from? What are we hiding? When things are too complicated it's because something's off! It's a sign you're not rightly aligned, that you're not flowing or living the fullness of life (John 10:10). I see a lot of stunted growth or no growth at all, and marriage and relationships are part of growth. You want to grow, but you don't live right. What are you expecting?

Let's start by taking a hard reality check, by asking ourselves some hard questions (I encourage you to answer honestly from your heart). Say the first thing that comes to your mind, not the trained "religious" answer. God can't steer a parked car, but has to first dislodge it. Get out of inaction (which starts in stuck thinking) and start moving. Honest answers are a great first step:

Questions to Ask Yourself:
- Is marriage really better than singleness?
- If I met the right person, would I be open to it?

- Is it possible the right person (or a good candidate) could be in my sphere, and I haven't considered it?
- Am I open to marriage, truly open?
- What is holding me back from dating and from marriage?
- What would help me be more ready? Is it a heart issue, lifestyle issue, attitude, unfaced fears and disappointment, or something else?
- What is one positive change I could make to cooperate with Jesus in this?
- What do my closest friends and pastor say about my readiness to get married? Have I asked, or allowed them to ask me, hard questions, or asked them to ask me hard questions? Have I taken an honest look in the mirror and invited their feedback? (If not, this could be good step to take!)

Now, let's face some of the most common fears. Some of these will surprise you, but I think if you peel back the layers (and cut through the rhetoric), you will see these fears are more prvelant than you may have first thought:

ΔRE YOU REALLY SCARED OF?

—That God won't give you a good mate?

—That marriage won't work for you?

—That it will crimp your style or keep you from achieving your goals?

—That you'll be abused or fall into the abusive patterns you saw at home?

—That it will curb your freedom?

—That there will be less fun?

—That you'll have to give up porn or other addictions?

—That it's more effort than it's worth?

—That God doesn't really love you or want you to be happy?

—That God wants you to be alone?

Actually face your fears. Actually list or speak them out. Say them to another person, to yourself, and even back to God. *Actually do this.* You need to hear it with your own voice. Then begin to ask yourself, "Is this rational?" "Does this make sense?" "Do I actually believe this, that God wants me to be single or doesn't love me enough to give me a mate? Or that I'm unworthy or unsuited for marriage?"

I've found that most fear is false evidence appearing real (F.E.A.R). I can't take credit for that acronym, but it is true in most of my life. Something fear does is that it becomes an emotion or even a spirit, which the Bible talks about (see 2 Timothy 1:7). Rarely is fear rational, and even more rarely is it truthful. Therefore, I've found it extremely important to get the fear out or answer the question, "What am I actually afraid of?" When you experience fear, stop for a moment and say, "OK, what am I actually afraid of? What could happen, or what is it that I want (or don't want)? What do I believe, about God, myself, or others?"

Then, armed with this information, you can make or begin to make a rational decision, one based on logic. Are these fears for real? Are they truthful, rational, and likely to pan out? Or is it just the emotion and thought that is scaring me, but they're not really reality? Have I bought into lies or myths that simply aren't true, even if there's a powerful emotion attached to it?

This can go a long way in dispelling the very real fears that so many of us face. This is a difficult and rigorous process, but it gets easier once you get into it and is actually quite freeing. It's sort of a mini deliverance session on yourself! I highly encourage you to do it and make it a regular habit, particularly if you're someone like me who struggles, or has struggled, with fear.

Another thing I've seen evangelical singles do is become super fixated on marriage because they're afraid of getting hurt. Now it's good to be marriage-minded. I've always advocated dating with marriage in mind, particularly if it's anything beyond a few "get-to-know-you" dates. Long-term casual dating is not the thing, but we've taken a good thing and turned it into a vehicle for fear where out of fear all we can think about is marriage but none of the steps needed to get there. That's why we have these unrealistic expectations about falling in love and no clue what it will actually take, including basic steps like saying 'hello' or going on a first date.

That also explains the "freak out" when someone does say, "Hello," or asks you on a date. It's not a promise of marriage and it's not intended to be.

In some Christian circles, it's like we've retreated so far from the casual dating and hook-up culture that it's marriage or bust. This is unhelpful and unhealthy, not to mention unrealistic, and it's made a generation not more holy but more lonely, desperate, and hopeless about actually getting married. When something has had the opposite of the intended effect, it's probably worth examining if it is a good practice to continue doing!

I know a woman who didn't date out of college for FOURTEEN YEARS! She was convinced God was going to give her a husband, and a boatload of prophetic dreams and visions in advance so that she would know it. While I totally respect her not wanting to fool around or go from relationship to relationship (and I do believe God can speak to you about your future spouse), she now admits she was primarily motivated by fear. It may look holy, but God can't bless us when we're not walking in faith.

I remember saying back in college that I hoped the next girl I dated would be the one that I would marry, even when I knew that this was unlikely. I'm sure it can happen, but I could tell that what was behind my desire was not simply holiness but really a fear of getting hurt. A fear of taking chances. A fear of having to stand up as a man. And that's why God couldn't bless that desire, no matter how much I prayed and tried to walk it out.

My friend who waited 14 years eventually got married in her mid-thirties, but it hasn't been a cakewalk. The waiting allowed her to travel, do ministry, and get financially stable, but it didn't guarantee a perfect marriage. It also limited the number of children she was able to have.

When our desires are rooted in sin, or are a way of camouflaging sin, we are fighting God. God's desire is to reveal and illuminate our sins, not to shame us but to get them out of us. If you're not partnering with God in that then you are resisting him. And then we wonder why the blessings aren't flowing.

MY "ERIC" STORY

There was a time in my life when I was working a full-time job, had earned my degree, owned a car, had a good living arrangement, and money in the bank. I wasn't involved in blatant sin or addiction (like porn, drugs, etc.). I wore decent clothes, went to church multiple times a week, and had a group of friends, yet I couldn't get a date to save my life. Nothing was happening in my love life.

There didn't seem to be any prospects and no one who caught my eye, or whatever interests I had didn't seem to click with me, or vice versa. I was in a wilderness and stressed about it. Nothing was going right.

In this season, God sent "Eric." He had no car, no job, no college degree, no money in the bank, and was still maturing in his Christian walk. And yet, within a short amount of time, an attractive young woman from church with a college degree fell head-over-heels in love with him. They soon got married, started a family, and began their new life. How did this happen? What was I missing that Eric had?

Issues and all, Eric was OK with who he was. He wasn't pretending to be someone he wasn't. Honesty is very attractive, since you're going to be giving yourself to another person, and part of the point of marriage is to be known—a pretty big part, actually.

Eric's life and romantic success hit me pretty hard. God was showing me that I couldn't earn it. I thought I *deserved* a girl because of how awesome my life was, how I'd "made something of myself" professionally or paid my bills, bought a car, etc. All the things women are longing for, right? I was even proud of my "holy" living, having overcome my teenage struggle with porn. But the things I thought were so beautiful were repulsive to God, and to others, because they were clothed in pride.

If I'd found a spouse in that season it would have been the worst thing for me. It would have only bolstered my pride because "I earned it. I made it happen. I was right." I struggle enough with these thoughts as it is; I can only imagine how much worse it would have been for my wife if we had met and married in this stage (we very likely would not have gotten married). What a horrible foundation for a relationship.

This is probably why I had to wait through my thirties. It wasn't so much my life that I had to get in order but my pride, my false mindsets, and my behaviors. That's a big point in this book. Most people can tell you practical tips to prepare for marriage and a relationship—pay your bills, finish college, take daily showers, etc. They may even tell you to go to church or to address your sin issues (addictions, etc.). But very few will talk to the heart of issues like bitterness, pride, and disappointment, which I see as way more toxic than not having enough money in the bank or needing to lose a few pounds.

As humans, we are horrible sinners and we need an amazing (and complete) savior. Don't believe me, just read Romans 7, where Paul laments his battle with sin—this after encountering Jesus on the road to Damascus and writing much of the New Testament.

We tend to minimize and isolate sin but God has a much more complete view of it. He can see things the naked eye can't, like when we look through a microscope and see all the germs on a "clean" surface. Have you let God take a microscope to your life? Because sin and issues are there whether we see them or not. Jesus wants to free us so we can be fully happy in Him. Have you said "Yes" to that today?

SAY 'NO' TO FAIRYTALES

Maybe because my parents did not have a good marriage I've never believed in the fairytale picture of relationships. I've always known they are work, complicated, and robust. Not that there can't be honeymoon seasons and times of joy and bliss, but it's not a cakewalk. Now I often took this to a negative extreme, making things super complicated and difficult, or, for a long time, believing that I couldn't be in a relationship until I'd worked through all of my issues. Eventually, you see this is exhausting and impossible. God will work with us, but we can do nothing apart from Him (John 15:5).

When Jesus said to love you neighbor as you love yourself, this is hard to do if you don't love yourself. That's a lot of what my issue was. Behind the success drive and hard work, even to get over my sin issues, was a rampant insecurity and dislike of self. Have you ever known those people that seem to have it all together, where their life appears to be well ordered but you know there's something off? There's something you can't spot or put your finger on, but you know it's there? That was me! Like I said, I checked all the boxes of car, job, church, cash, and "sinless" living, but I really didn't like myself or trust that anyone else would. I desperately wanted to be liked, and was looking for evidence that someone did, anyone really, yet I masked this with a tough, "I don't need anyone, I'm better than you," exterior. How disgusting! This was the sign above my head.

It's no wonder "Eric" got blessed and not me. His sign was clear: I'm a mess, but take me as I am. I've got some issues, but why wouldn't someone like me? I'm ready to move forward.

Instead of making someone climb through a maze of walls and qualifications, Eric lived his life openly, open to a relationship and blessing, while I sat back and judged him, myself, and others.

Because I'd disqualified myself, it was easier to disqualify others. Perhaps there were dateable women around, but I couldn't see them because I was focused on my faults, and theirs. If I wasn't good enough then they weren't either. Out of fear of rejection, I moved toward extremes: either she was out of my league, or totally beneath me and unworthy of my time or attention. It's gross, even as I write this, but that's how I lived—for years—out of fear and loneliness.

Has loneliness become a self-fulfilling prophecy? Have you taken on a false identity as that lonely, older single person? The not-yet-married thirty-something who just can't seem to find love? Is your heart starting to turn resentful and bitter, or has it already gone there? Don't waste another minute in bitterness and pride. You're not helping yourself or others, including the spouse that's trying to find you. Get alone with God. Seek counseling. Pray and repent. Do whatever is necessary. Don't spend another day with a closed and bitter heart. You'll be much more attractive without it—I promise!

Chapter 6

STOP BEING AFRAID (OF PEOPLE, GOD, AND YOURSELF)!

Oftentimes, if we've made it to our thirties single, it's because we're afraid of being who we really are and of submitting to another person. Many singles in their thirties have a deep fear of themselves and a fear of losing power and autonomy. Yet this is not biblical (your body belongs to your spouse once you're married, 1 Corinthians 7:4 says). It's also a camouflage for an extreme self-dislike. How many of us are hiding some level of self-hatred, self-doubt, or even self-loathing? It often manifests in a form of humility, one that can be endorsed in Christian circles but is ultimately quite unattractive. Not caring for yourself or paying attention to your needs is actually quite off-putting. Sure, the Bible instructs us to look out for others, but we are also to love each other as we love ourselves, and so without proper self-love we are rendered incapable of truly loving others. Letting people walk all over you in the name of serving them is also not love.

I hid this for years and it helped explain why I wasn't married. Oh sure, I was a great guy, very humble and even likable, but not romantically. Why? I had no confidence! I was hiding deep self-hatred, distrust, and depression. No wonder I couldn't get a date! So what if someone serves long hours and is gentle or kind; if they don't have confidence in themselves or don't like themselves deep down, it's not surprising that other people don't find them likable, either. Examine yourself and see if this is true for you.

ARE YOU OVER-DEVELOPING YOURSELF? (THE PERFECTION MYTH)

This usually comes out of brokenness and pain. If this is you, ask God to show you and to help you lose your taste for self-help, counseling, and even the inner healing and deliverance that can become addictions we hide behind as an excuse for not pursuing relationships. Let's face it: we're all looking for love and the goal of any of these healing programs is to enable you to give and receive love, from God and from others.

I'm all for working on yourself, and I've done most or all of the things I've mentioned above, plus 12-step recovery at one point for co-dependency. God wants us to work on ourselves but the truth is the work is never fully done. Some of that work is best done in a relationship, with a partner, someone to fight alongside you.

Now, don't just enter relationships full of blatant sin hoping that the other person will fix you. I don't recommend that, although sometimes God releases uncommon grace. Seek counsel if you believe that is God's will for your life. What I think is most helpful is to ask God what season you're in. I checked myself out of the dating scene in order to do 12-step recovery, and there have been seasons where I knew I needed to give my time to "working on my stuff," not to pursuing another person. But these were seasons, not a lifetime of dwelling on how much I needed to grow or change. It can help to have a goal in sight: 'I'm doing 12-step recovery (or counseling, inner healing or deliverance) so I can have better relationships, including marriage.'

Marriage is perhaps God's greatest growth agent for us. I don't recommend entering it with a broken leg and open wound about to bleed out, but if you've turned the corner and are in recovery (making active improvement) from your issues, then sharing that journey with someone can be invigorating. Again, begin with the end in mind.

One last note: If you find yourself attracted to someone who has lots of issues, and you still want to proceed, consider if praying for and supporting them, but not dating them, is best for that season. Some people want to be another's savior, but that is not a sustainable foundation for a relationship. Jesus Christ is, and wants to be, our only foundation. As a recovering co-dependent, I urge you to examine yourself and your motives, both for seeking inner healing, and for wanting to get involved in someone else's journey. This can be done purely, but it is very easy to take on for selfish gain.

Do You Really Want a Man?

I see some single women and question if they really want a man. What I mean by that is they either seem so content in their single life, or so resistant to the idea of being with a man and entering a marriage relationship. In other words, they portray being so hard to reach or that they're disinterested in a relationship because they've either been hurt, or they want only serious pursuers. I completely understand that, but a high bar and closed spirit can get to the point where it's off-putting.

Sometimes I wonder if they're truly open to a relationship. Some women have chosen to go the route of independence and doing things on their own, even forming their own family through adoption or other means. Men can do the same, building a world around themselves in which they are confident, successful, and safe, and bringing another person into it is disruptive, threatening, and difficult, if not impossible.

That's what I mean by "Do you really want a man?" Some of these women seem so strong, confident, and independent, it's worth asking if they really want a man and the disruption he'll bring. Do you want a man and his challenge to the power dynamics and your authority and independence? I think equality has been a great contribution to women in our society but at times has gone too far. Let me explain.

My wife is strong, competent, skilled, and independent. That's why I married her! She's not needy in that sense of the word. And yet she totally wanted to be in a relationship. That's what made her so attractive. A beautiful and competent woman who wanted to be around men, get to know them and ultimately be in a marriage relationship with a man. She was willing to take the steps necessary, including having an open heart and building good relationships with members of the opposite sex, and ultimately being open to my pursuit of her.

I fear that some women have either set the bar so high, built a fortress around themselves, or bought so heavily into society's lines about liberation and independence that there's little room for a guy to get in. Again, I'm all for women's independence, but when taken to an extreme it can be difficult to shift course to being in a mutual, marriage relationship. Some of this includes putting men down or always finding fault with them and acting like they're not good enough. I'm all for women having high esteem of themselves and not just taking any guy that comes along. But again, we're talking about extremes and attitudes that I've seen that are preventing some women from even entering into relationships, or guys from wanting to pursue them for a relationship.

It's like their door is already closed. They're projecting that they don't really want a man, or that only when the perfect man shows up and does everything right to conquer their walls will they open up. (For some, I think that if Jesus Himself touched down and asked to marry them they'd still have to go think about it!). Now again, I'm all for men pursuing, but sometimes these women aren't helping by the attitude or expression on their face or their lifestyle.

Ask yourself these questions: Are you really open to a man? Is a man what you want? Knowing that he's not perfect, knowing that he'll be disruptive, knowing the power dynamics may shift or that he'll bring his faults into the relationship. Can you handle that? Are you ready for that? Are two really better than one or do you prefer to go it on your own? This issue must be dealt with in order to move forward. Otherwise, it's blissful dreaming.

KEEPING YOUR HEART UNOFFENDED

Now, men *and* women, this section is for you…

When you wait patiently with an unoffended heart, it's easy for God to do quick work, a 'suddenly,' and fulfill your dream (and His). I see it all around me, people who walked humbly with God, not hiding or counting themselves out (although there may have been moments) but they stayed in faith, confident that God would bless them. They didn't fall into bitterness, inaction, or unbelief, but dwelt in the grace given to them, knowing that their breakthrough was ahead. "As a man sows, so shall he reap" (Galatians 6:7). It's *impossible* to sow to the kingdom and not reap. Hebrews 11:6 tells us that "God rewards those who diligently seek Him," but we must be worshipping Him in Spirit and in truth, as Jesus says in John 4:24. That's why lies are not welcome.

Some of you need to sow some different seeds than the ones you've been sowing. If you're not seeing a harvest, sometimes the problem is with the seed. It's either with the seed or the soil (sometimes it's the sower, but I think we've dealt enough with that). You may say, "But I'm always at church, in prayer, in Bible study, etc. Why am I not seeing a harvest?" Perhaps there's mixture. Alongside your "good" seed of prayer and Scripture study are seeds of pride, bitterness, disappointment, and resentment. That being the case, God can't bless you like He desires. If your motives are off then your fruit will be too. "No good tree can bear bad fruit, and no bad tree can bear good fruit," Matthew 7:18 says. "You shall know a tree by its fruit," Jesus warns in Matthew 7:16.

If you've been praying, fasting, and crying out and you haven't seen a harvest, perhaps you're not praying right, or maybe you're not as holy as you think. We all tend to overestimate our own goodness and holiness, yet if we take an honest look into Scripture, and at our sinless Lord and King, His Spirit will tell us the truth. Jesus *is* the Truth, and His Spirit is the Spirit of Truth (John 14:6).

Chapter 7

EYES & SIGNS

What Do Your Eyes Say? You may have heard it said that, "The eyes are the windows to the soul." If that's true, what do your eyes say? Are they bright or dim? Open or closed? Strong or weak? The Bible talks about this when comparing Rachel's and Leah's eyes (Genesis 29:16-17).

It says that Leah's eyes were soft or weak (and also soft or weak to look at), in contrast with Rachel, who was "beautiful in form *and* appearance." Appearance probably means the look in her eye, the grin on her face, the power with which she walked. Her form was her physical body. Shape is attractive, but a woman's appearance (how she carries herself, how she talks and looks you in the eye) makes all the difference.

When a woman looks like she's going to reject you before you speak, that's not a good sign. Attractive women must keep some guard—they don't want every single guy approaching them— but they're open to quality suitors and respectful approaches (which they can decline or accept).

A real woman is secure enough in herself to be friendly or open at the start, and then quickly close or dismiss as needed. This is the grace or "princess" anointing (royal, really) we see so often on film, that a woman of great stature and beauty who is also kind and approachable to those beneath her. Sure, her close associates are those with similar interests or social class, but she is not cruel or condescending to those beneath her. True beauty doesn't condescend or put others down. Instead, it lifts them up and shines light on them. Which kind of woman are you?

THE SIGN ABOVE YOUR HEAD

What does it say? What is the word written above your head? What signal are you giving off or message are you communicating? Because it's real. It exists, whether you recognize it or not. Others see it, and in particular others of the opposite sex. Often or very quickly, they can key in on what the message above your head is much faster than you.

For example, some people's signs say 'Bitter.' 'Angry.' 'Closed.' Or 'Suspicious.' 'Hurt.' Others are 'Easy.' 'Open.' 'Desperate.' For some it's 'Insecure.' 'Inferior.' 'Unsure.'

What are you giving off about yourself? What do you believe and feel about yourself, as well as what do you think about relationships in general? This is the sign above your head. If you've been a long time without a relationship or had trouble finding a good one, you might want to check what your sign says. Unsure of what it is? Try asking those closest to you or those that know you best. If that's too vulnerable, ask a friend or co-worker; someone whose opinion won't wreck you if it's critical.

I've seen so many people, out of the pain or disappointment of not dating or finding someone, begin to close their hearts. Then they wonder why they can't find anyone. Bitterness rarely brings blessing, and the Bible is stern in its warnings about how it can defile, contaminate, and bring all kinds of destruction. So do jealousy and envy, or jealous envy (the book of James contains some stern warnings). I submit that for a good number of us, if you've made it to your thirties you're probably dealing with one or more of these things; and it's better to contend with it, recognize it, and repent than to keep going on blaming others, denying it, or just hoping things will get better. Confrontation brings blessing if you're confronting lies!

One of the things that really stood out to me about my wife was that she wasn't bitter. She also wasn't closed to the idea of dating or marriage, or having a good relationship. She didn't count herself out thinking that she was unworthy or that it wouldn't happen. Rather, she continued in faith and prayed, and even fasted, until she eventually found a husband.

Now she did have a time of mourning and dealing with stuff with the Lord after the breakup of her last relationship. She didn't just go straight into a new one. But after that season of wrestling and giving herself and her desires over to Jesus, she was ready to enter into a good relationship when it came along.

Another thing she did is she never tried to deny that she wanted to get married. She didn't try to hide it, even though she had past pain and disappointments, and never entered that in-between land of claiming she didn't want it when she really did or pretending like all men are bad and there's no good ones out there. Rather, she continued in faith and the simple expectation that God would provide a good husband, her past experience notwithstanding. Even sin from her past relationships didn't disqualify her from the love and blessing of her Father. Her faith was well rewarded.

How much baggage are you carrying around? How much guilt or shame are you carrying from past failures in relationships, or even just the shame of being single in your thirties? Have you recognized that you have these things? Do you want to keep them? Are they helping or hurting your chances of actually getting into the kind of relationship and marriage that you want? These are fair questions.

IMAGINARY RELATIONSHIP PROBLEMS

I mentioned earlier that I met a guy who was turning forty and had just gotten out of a three-year relationship. I'm like, *"Really*? At your age and stage of life, you should be dating for marriage and it shouldn't take more than one or two years *max* to figure out if she's the right one."

I didn't ask more specifics, like if there was distance involved, but my general outlook is you should be dating for marriage, and the more mature and healed you are, the more quickly you should be able to determine if he or she is the one —not leading someone on for two-plus years.
We've already spoken about the "quick" timeline my wife and I courted and married. What we

didn't have was a protracted season of figuring out if we liked each other, wanted to get married, or were interested in marriage in the first place. At our age and stage (me early forties and her early thirties) we were both marriage-minded. We'd both come out of seasons of dealing with our personal brokenness (hers was right before we met; mine was during the time that we met). We clicked, got along well, and enjoyed each other's company the more we experienced it. Even our first "date" lasted about an hour and a half longer than planned because we just kept talking.

That's part of what clued me in that this girl was something special. Instead of things getting tense or awkward, it seemed the more we talked, the more we flowed. It wasn't difficult or stilted, and we could have kept talking longer. Four years later, we're still talking! The switch flipped, the lightbulb turned on, and I began to pursue her, knowing from the start this was a rare connection and could actually be serious.

Did I know everything about her? No. Had I met her family? (No, they live out of the country.) Did she understand everything about my life and career? (I'm a writer and missionary.) Did we have every question answered about our future? No! What we did have was a genuine affection and bond, along with a conviction that two are better than one, that we would prefer to face life together than alone. It's still true today.

WARNING SIGNS

I've seen men spin, and I've spun, the most elaborate tales of how I'm going to get a girl and how God is going to intervene, change her heart and bring us together, forever. I'm even feeling a bit sick as I write this! How did we go from pursuing to believing in fantasies that are as bad, or worse, than a Hollywood movie? C'mon, guys! Romantic fantasy is typically what they sell to women, who are commonly waiting or believing for their prince to come, but now men are susceptible. And it seems increasingly common with Christian men.

It looks so holy, so honorable, so manly even, but it's usually bankrupt. Ever heard phrases like this? "She doesn't like me, but I'll win her heart."

"We're not talking, but she'll come aroun broke up (seven years ago!), but she'll come to me." It's usually all bunk!

A safe rule of thumb is how much are you talking now? How much relationship exists in real life (not in your head)? Does she actually like you (and you her), in real life? What kind of relationship do you actually have? The less that's going on in this department, even if it's not romantic, the more skeptical I am.

Now, you're probably thinking of friend or a story you heard about God changing someone's heart, or a guy pursuing a girl through different waves of rejection. I have too. And I believe them. The one common thing I've seen is that there was relationship to start with. God doesn't violate a person's free will. He's not going to make someone like you that doesn't. He may reveal things to a person or help open their eyes, for instance, but I don't see Him changing someone's tastes or affections in an instant (this is a general rule, not hard and fast—I'm not going to put God in a box. He's God, after all).

to persist then there will

ut if you're coming up

on. Even if you move on

it fantasy girl is actually

..........y—I believe God will graciously
correct you. He wants good relationships, after
all. But I can't justify wasting years of your life,
and your mental (and spiritual) attention,
focused on something that isn't working out.
God gives good gifts. He's a gracious giver. We
don't have to wrestle blessings out of His hand.

HOW TO KNOW IF YOUR ROMANTIC FANTASY IS DEAD (OR DYING)

It's like the guy who watches porn instead of
pursuing a woman. Would you rather talk *about*
your girl, or actually talk *to* her? When this stays
out of whack, or never gets off the ground in the
first place, then your fantasy is likely dead.

The times I've seen it work is when two people
had a relationship, romantic or otherwise; one
person liked the other and the other one didn't,
was scared to admit it, or needed time to come to

the same conclusion. Eventually, through trial and error and much prayer, they came around and a healthy relationship (usually ending in marriage) ensued. Winning hearts is godly; fantasizing about them is not.

LOVE OR THE IDEA OF LOVE?

There's an old rock song that has a great line in it: "Was it love, or was it the idea of being in love?" I think this applies to most romantic dreamers, of either sex, but particularly men. Afraid of actual relationships, including the hard work and risk of rejection or failure, we create a safe fantasy world of what we want love to be like. "When she comes around, we're going to do x y z." "Once we get married it will be like ..." "God's going to move her heart and we're going to ..."

The times where I saw God move, the men in particular were in fear or awe, not prideful confidence. In other words, they believed that God was helping (or going to help) bring the woman around, but they largely had no idea how that would happen. And they were in awe when it did, pleasantly surprised when they asked again (usually following the prompting of the Spirit) and this time she said, "Yes!" There was no prideful boasting ahead of time but a sincere, humble walking with God toward what they believed He had for them. This is glorious, and these stories I love retelling.

One guy asked his wife something like three or four times before she said 'yes'; another guy got a deadline from the Lord and, a few weeks shy of it, the woman did a complete 180 and admitted she was in love with him. These are very far from the puffed-up, and usually imaginary, tales that desperate men spin to conceal their loneliness and lack of confidence (and lack of faith in themselves).

BREAKING (FALSE) PROPHETIC NARRATIVES

The devil loves to hide in the church! He loves to use the very real gift of prophecy to steal kill and destroy. The gift is meant to edify, exhort, and encourage, but kudos to him if he can get it to confuse, delay, and destroy lives. While not all prophetic narratives are bad, the flesh has a sneaky way of getting in and changing, or altering, what God might actually be saying. This can happen when we have a fleshly response to a real word from God.

For example, God once told me crystal clear that something big would happen on a certain date. I was pursuing a young woman at the time so I instantly assumed it meant something would happen with her, or me and her. I was wrong! God *DID* do something important on that day, but it had *nothing* to do with her. Yet, because I heard the word so clearly about the date, I told as many people as possible that she would be coming around on that date. This was pride. Again, the word was true, but my fleshly interpretation of it was not.

We all want to avoid suffering, but a prophetic narrative misapplied will only increase it. Remember,

The human heart is exceedingly wicked
and who can know its depths? (Jeremiah 17:9)

—And when prophecy is used for hiding our fears and insecurities, God can rarely bless it.

Are You Using Prayer as a Cop-Out?

I was using prayer as a cop-out because I didn't want to take action. I wanted God to do all the work. I was asking people to pray for me to get married or to find a spouse because I didn't want to do anything about it. I was unwilling, or felt unable, to take the necessary steps to find a spouse, so I reasoned that if I kept praying, or got enough people to pray, somehow it would magically happen. Prayer without repentance is rarely the point. God wasn't denying me a good gift, but he wanted me to change some things about my attitude, heart, and what I was believing.

The Lord wasn't denying my request because he didn't want to grant it, but He was after something different than just racking up more and more people to pray and then "boom," marriage. Again, in my experience God rarely works like this. He cares about the whole person, including the bad things that we believe or that we don't like ourselves, or any other number of dysfunctions that are holding us back as much if not more than lack of a good marriage candidate.

Let's get honest with ourselves, with God, and with others and stop using prayer as a cop-out. Again, I am a fan of prayer, but if you've been praying and asking people to pray and you're not seeing any results, and you also haven't changed any of your actions, maybe it's time to re-examine the fruit of your prayers.

You can ask God, "Is there anything else you want me to do besides just pray and ask more people to pray?" He may say, "No, everything's fine" and that He's going to bring the blessing, or the blessing is on its way, and I can believe that, but I would need reassurance from the Lord. If I was praying and not seeing any results, I would encourage you to check in and ask, "God is this really your plan for me, or are there other things I need to do or add to my prayers?" I'm not anti-prayer (I've been part of a 24/7 prayer ministry for more than a decade), but I believe, and we see in biblical examples, that our prayers are to be backed with godly action in almost all cases.

ARE YOU USING SPIRITUALITY AS A COP-OUT?

I once asked a friend in his thirties what he wanted for his birthday. His answer was something cryptic like, "For the prophets to arise." I said, "That's great. How about for you?" He couldn't give an answer. Sure, I want the prophets to arise. I pray for an outpouring of God's prophetic spirit on all flesh, like what is quoted in Acts 2. But a single man in his thirties should have desires, one of them being to get married. A few months later, this same guy moved cross-country to pursue a woman he had met, proving that marriage was on his mind.

What is up with our vagueness? Why are we afraid (or unable) to give honest answers? I'm not saying to walk around with a bullhorn announcing to everyone that we want to get married, but why not to those close to us, those we have relationship with who actually care about us? I understand guarding your heart but it can be a warning sign when someone is keeping things completely hidden.

This was a breakthrough for me when I hit forty. I could no longer hide and couch my answers behind spirituality, busyness, etc. I was single because I didn't want to be married at that point, or I couldn't bring myself to face my desires (and fears) and state them openly. I was scared. At forty, I had run out of excuses and I had to confess that my biological clock, even as a man, was starting to tick. I had lived enough of life and done and seen enough things that there was nothing else for me to claim I was delaying marriage for. At this point, I began confessing that I wanted to get married. I pursued one relationship shortly after I turned forty, and then met my wife when I was forty-one.

Now, don't just go telling everyone you know. Use discernment. But stop hiding, denying, and lying, acting like it is no big deal. God takes you seriously and "the power of life and death is in the tongue" (Proverbs 18:21), so, why not speak what you want? You might just see fruit! ("As a man sows, so he shall reap," Galatians 6:7 says, and our words are a big part of that).

Chapter 8

It's Your Belief, Not Your Circumstances!

We claim it's money, our job, or not enough good options, but truly it's an issue of belief: Do you believe you're destined to get married, and is God leading you toward finding your mate (and are you cooperating with His leadership through prayer and godly action)?

It's like the Christian journey toward heaven. We believe God is guiding us there and that we will get there, even if there's no daily evidence (and sometimes contra-evidence) that we are getting closer to it. We cling to that hope, even on our worst days, and are secure in our destiny. Some days it prompts us to work harder, pray or keep on in the fight. This belief guides our actions and provides an overall framework for our life: we are heaven-bound. Indeed, we already belong to it because we are in Christ, even if we are waiting for it to manifest.

Yes, it can be the same with marriage! If you believe God has marriage for you then you can start living, acting, and preparing mentally and in righteous deeds for the day it manifests. Having a clear goal and overriding mindset is helpful. I believe God will give marriage to almost anyone that desires it—if we will partner with him by renouncing bad beliefs, attitudes and behaviors and position ourselves through some basic preparation.

Real marriage is worth it—a true gift from God. Start thanking Him for it, believing that He doesn't want to withhold this gift from you but bless you abundantly. Jesus offers life to the full (John 10:10). It is difficult to experience this fullness of life independent of marriage (there are some who have that grace, but very few, and, of course, those who are poorly married have other challenges).

This bedrock belief that God has marriage for you and will bring it to you, and you to it, can help once you are married. Challenges are sure to come in even the best of marriages. Having it set in your mind that God intends for you to get married and stay married can help you persevere when things are tough. If things come too easily we tend to take them for granted. Some amount of struggle is good, but I'm calling you to "fight the good fight" of faith, not the self-destructive and bitter journey some of us are on. If that's you, repent today! Jesus' blood covers all sin.

Is It The Poverty Mindset?

Ever heard the line that "There's only so many Christian men or women to go around," so it's harder to find a mate? Do we lie to ourselves and say that we're stuck because there just aren't as many choices as in the world? This has even caused some women to go seek a spouse in the world or to date worldly men (and often fall into temptation or sin). I'm not unaware of the number dynamics—is God? And can He not do anything at any time, like saving someone, moving someone to a new city, or opening someone's eyes or heart to consider a prospective mate? Sometimes He'll speak to another person to help make a connection we didn't know about or see before. He's an excellent matchmaker!

None of these complaints are a good reason for sin or for unbelief. Let's stop accusing God by just stating a bunch of statistics as justification for our bad attitude, inaction, or other sinful patterns that we perpetuate. God wants you married and if you're willing to cooperate it will happen.

I heard of a woman recently who had been praying for YEARS for a husband. A good man finally showed up and began to pursue her but she wanted to break up with him because he wasn't "spiritual enough," even though he was trying to grow in the Lord. Another lady in her 50s confided in me that the moment any man shows interest in her she instantly becomes critical of him. There *ARE* good men (and good women) out there, but the junk in our hearts keeps us from seeing or accepting them!

If marriage is a priority, prioritize it. Yes, the Lord is our first priority, but if you desire the gift of marriage and believe God has it for you, why not pursue it much like you would any other gift? Don't make an idol out of it but act in faith. Examine your heart to clean up any baggage or false beliefs. Say your prayers (including thankfulness for the amazing spouse God has for you!), tell a few friends and consider even doing some fasting. Fasting doesn't twist God's arm but is a demonstration that we're serious. It puts 'feet' to our prayers, usually causes a spiritual increase, and can allow God to bring up some issues or barriers that wouldn't come to light unless we strip away the comfort of food (For some resources on fasting, see Appendix B).

You know what makes a guy or girl attractive? Confidence! It's that they're open but not too needy. Enthusiastic without being clingy. Pursuing but not addicted. Don't only think "Where can I find one of these," but, "How can I *be* one of these?" Or ask yourself, "*Am I one of these?* Do these attributes describe me? In my heart of hearts, what do I think about myself, God, and relationships? Am I mature and ready enough to be in one (and *WANT*) to be in one?"

Who knows, you may end up talking yourself into it just by answering these questions!

I got excited when I met my wife (or started pursuing her). It was an exciting time when I realized this could be serious, that she actually could be "the one." And yet, there was a tempered sobriety because she could really be my marriage partner. Sure, there's always a "rose colored glasses" phase in most relationships, but beyond the inevitable flutter of positive emotions I was able, and we were able, to evaluate one another's suitedness for marriage and for each other.

Marriage is giving yourself to another person, not hiding yourself. That's why all this hiding and denying has got to stop. If you're doing it, stop being part of the problem. The more confident you are in yourself the more you can give yourself to someone else. The more you know yourself—in a healthy way, not endless introspection—the more prepared you are for the pitfalls of a relationship, and the more you can spot if one isn't working out!

Pay attention to this! If you're changing and it's not for the better, something's wrong. This includes falling into sins like drug use and premarital sex.

I just heard a great quote that a whole man wants a whole woman, and this is true. Maybe the fact that I couldn't get a date or spark friendships with normal, whole women communicated more about me than it did them. Why were no "normal" girls attracted to me, but only those with lots of issues? Maybe it's because I had lots of issues! Why were things always complicated and confusing, or dramatic? Maybe it's because I was complicated, confused, and dramatic (at that stage). The breakthrough lay in me, not outside of me. It wasn't the women that needed to change or become something different, it was me that needed to change.

Chapter 9

THE REVEALING OF DESIRES

Often, people are addicted to how it's going to happen: How will I meet my spouse? But you must make an effort once you've decided you're ready to meet your mate. Go on a blind date, join a dating site, visit a different church, ask specific people to pray for you. You've got to up your faith and believe God while keeping Him in first place. Sometimes, He won't answer right away, and it's rarely on our timetable, but I and many others have experienced a breakthrough at the appointed time. I had to seek Him in the "lean" years, when I had no dating prospects or specific hope of getting married. I couldn't see the way but I kept pursuing Him because He *is* "the Way" (John 14:6).

God can do more in five seconds than I can in my entire lifetime. He can break any chain, move a person, or change a heart. It doesn't take much for Him; He's often waiting on us to be ready!

I've heard it said that sometimes God is waiting to tell us His will until we're ready to receive it. In other words, if He told us now we'd refuse, cower in fear, or go into outright rebellion and unbelief. It takes much humbling for some of us to reach the end of our rope and really lay down our lives, but isn't this what God wants (Romans 12:1-2)? He's chosen the foolish things of the world to shame the wise. Can we stop being so wise in our own eyes?

PRAYING WITH EXPECTATION

Some Christian's don't even have to pray that much about their future spouse. They go through life confident that God loves them, they're blessed, enough (or worthy), and that God will bring good things to them. Some call this the "health and wealth" gospel, but I see it as part of the true gospel. We *ARE* loved, cherished and blessed. We are the head, not the tail. Will we walk in it and not our fears, doubts or restrictions? There's certainly a fault of believing that God is *only* health, wealth and prosperity. He allows lean times to grow and refine us, but fundamentally, He's good and working all things for our good (Romans 8:28). Can we agree on that?

Sometimes I'm judging if a person is really free. Do they move free, live free, talk free, and relate freely, as in unencumbered? Do they appear unburdened, un awkward and unrestricted? These are the real tests. And when the answer is "No," there's usually something wrong. That's the tell. If the person is not simple, clean, and clear relationally, then something's amiss. I'm not talking about personality (some people are more extroverted than others, for instance) but the feeling that you get when you interact with them, spend time with them, and think about them.

Many times it's intangible, but if there isn't peace, joy, and happiness then something's off.

Some friends of mine were adopting a child. It was their second adoptive daughter, and as can often happen with adoptions, there were some questions about whether one or both of the birthparents would sign the appropriate papers or would object to the adoption in anyway. They were experiencing some pushback and so they asked me to pray that everything would go smoothly in the procedure. Now that sounds innocent enough, but they were knee-deep in the process and were at the final stage of getting their daughter. All they had to do was clear this final hearing and the girl would be theirs.

I asked them a straight up question: "Do you believe this is your daughter?"

"Yes," they answered. Then I said, "I'm not going to pray for you, but simply thank God and declare that she is yours. It makes no sense to beg God or petition Him for things that you believe He's already given you. If you believe this is your daughter, and all the signs seem to line up that way (God has lead you to her and aligned every other part of the situation to make it clear that this is the girl for you and you're the family for her), then I'm going to believe Him to carry through to the end whatever paperwork or court order is needed to finish that process."

Now, of course, you may have some instance pop in your mind where you got 90% through something and then it fell apart. And I'm sure these things can happen, but I'm not going to pray that way or live in the space of the "what-ifs." Rather, all the signs seemed to align and these are godly, prayerful people, so I knew that they weren't acting on a selfish whim or just making this up. After hours of prayer and their own sacrifice they were on the brink of adopting a child. Next time I saw them they were holding their second beautiful adopted baby girl!

When I finally clicked and connected with my wife, I began to believe pretty quickly that she was the one for me to marry. I actually prayed about it surprisingly little because it wasn't that hard to see. All the prayers I prayed, all the long nights, all the desperate moves I made to try to end my singleness, and all the faking and dumb things I tried actually prepared me in this case to spot the real thing. I didn't have to pray long hours or go on a 40-day fast to figure out if I liked this girl and if she seemed to like me too and if we were compatible.

Give yourself some credit! Perhaps all the prayers you prayed really do work and are working to get you closer to your goal. It's yourself that's in doubt or unbelief. God is good. He never forgets a prayer and He does want to answer and give us the desires of our heart as we delight in Him (Psalm 37:4). Step back and ask yourself, if someone came to you and said they had prayed hours and hours and asked God earnestly for something and then they began to see signs that it was getting answered, would you encourage them to believe that it was God? In most cases I would say 'yes,' particularly if you knew they were praying for something good and praying with pure motives.

Why is it so validating that we remain in such a strong unbelief, forever wavering and questioning if it's really God? I think it's because it's an area we are so insecure about. And by area I mostly mean ourselves, although society has not helped with our pictures of marriage and relationships. Marriage is a good thing, and if you truly believe God has it for you, then that should change how you pray. And that should spark faith or build faith that God is answering the prayers you pray, even if you're in a wilderness.

As I've said, my wife and I went from met to married in eleven months, and I had very few encouraging signs in the lead-up to our romance. In fact, I was in the worst or one of the worst emotional seasons of my life. Yet, somehow, God was edging me closer to the goal and still very much wanting to give me the desires of my heart, and hers. He hadn't changed, given up, or quit, even though I had or was tempted to many times.

Sometimes, you have to step back and look at yourself from an outside perspective. That's what good friends and relationships do for us. They often call us on our junk or talk sense into us. Oftentimes other people will believe in us before we believe in ourselves, or they will have faith for us when we struggle to have faith for ourselves. This is partly why God designed us for community. And in most other cultures, dating and relationship decisions are made in a community, or with heavy input from a community.

Now, of course, I don't just share my business with everyone. It's important to guard your heart and the heart of the person you're pursuing, but share with a few trusted friends, counselors, an older couple, pastor, or whatever it takes. What I'm basically saying is having people who believe in you and can also talk sense and reality into you is key. We're not made to do it on our own or figure these things out completely apart from others. Marriage is a partnership, and it often takes partnership with godly people to help us get there. This is part of God's design. And one reason is, you will almost certainly need godly people in your life once you are married in order to have a good marriage and stay on the road that God has prepared for you. It does truly take a village! Or at least a team. This is another obstacle in our independent American culture.

If you have nothing to hide, you'll move forward. If there's nothing holding you back, you'll take action. And if there's nothing inhibiting you, you'll be ready when action comes or to receive appropriate overtures of romantic attention. The less clutter in your life, the clearer and easier the process will be (I've seen both males and females build such elaborate walls and structures around themselves that it would be difficult, yeah, impossible for someone of the opposite sex to break in! Like I said earlier, I think some women are waiting for Jesus Himself, and even then it would be a 'maybe').

This is a call for people to be a little more normal. Yes, steward God's call on your life; don't sacrifice that for anything. But be aware if you consciously or subconsciously create an idol or include barriers and requirements that God Himself did not stipulate, even when He called you to Himself or to a special work. Have you added on to the prophecy or prophetic word that you received? This is very common and difficult to spot. You could be doing good things that are the enemy of best. You could be walking in one grace while denying another grace that God wants to give you. Don't stay in fear, doubt, or unbelief. It's not that holy.

I was hiding, living in people's basements, and seeking other family because I was scared to have my own! I desperately wanted the benefits of family without having to pay the price for family. This is the mark of a boy, not man, wanting the benefit without paying the price, trying to get something for nothing, or, even worse, the appearance that you've got something when you don't. (Think about the problem with porn and what it's done for society.)

We're designed for the closeness and nearness that family affords, but we don't want to follow God's way to get it (marriage and family). Again, we're mad at God at the end of the day, denying His will and His ways and the systems He's set up (or allowed to be set up). We don't like His choices and His ways because we don't like Him.

We may not even like our gender! I covered this in my section, Do You Really Want a Man? One reason you may not find yourself attracted to the opposite sex is because you've been hurt by them at some point. Check yourself. Is there something keeping you from the right relationships?

ACTION STEP: START ADMITTING YOU WANT TO GET MARRIED!

Once I turned forty, it was time to let the cat out of the bag. I was still afraid and insecure about marriage, but one of my most significant excuses was now gone. What was I really waiting for? Maybe it was time to finally be in a hurry. I'd also done enough of life to realize something was still missing. I knew that more ministry, money, travel or experiences wouldn't fulfill the aching desire for partnership, even if I was afraid of it in some ways (not trusting myself, for instance).

I began to change my speech and my actions. I started telling people, within reason, that I *did* want to get married. I began to speak it out, timidly at first, but at least I was saying it. I pursued one relationship, which was a failure, went into the most intense depression of my life for several months (it's like being disappointed by your first meal after being stranded in the wilderness), experienced dramatic healing from God, and, within a few weeks was dating my wife.

I remember our first long conversation, the one that "opened my eyes" that she could be "the one" and caused me to start pursuing her. In that conversation, I asked, "What do you want in this season of life?' I don't remember exactly what she answered (it was probably more of the Lord, or something like that), but then she asked me. In an honest and not creepy way I said, "I want to get married and have kids."

I stole this answer from a friend who used to work for a major television network. She had achieved success but was tiring of her career and desired a family. When asked for her goals for the next year on her performance review, she said, "I want to get married and have kids." This wasn't what her boss wanted to hear, but she insisted because it was true. Not long after that, she met a friend of mine, got married and they have a beautiful family today.

I put it out there. It's not wrong, particularly as a thirty-plus adult, to be upfront about things. You *should* desire to get married. It's a natural desire that God gave us and one of His greatest gifts, and challenges, to mankind. The overwhelming majority of humans are meant to be married.

My answer came after a long, honest, and candid dialogue. It was near the end of our talk, long after we'd established trust and talked about many surface or lesser important, but still serious, things (I'm not one for petty small talk). We were bearing our hearts and talking honestly as one does to a friend (we we're already acquainted for several months before we had this conversation). It would have been completely different if I had started the conversation off with this (although, who knows?!). I was stating it as a matter of fact: this is where I'm at, someone who is looking to settle down and get married, not using it as a come on or pickup line. This honesty allowed me to get it right out on the table and opened the door for my wife to see me as a serious contender, not someone who's just playing around or out for a good time.

I think this is what women are looking for. They don't need the guy to be perfect, just honest. Just to man up. Just to get serious, put himself out there and pursue. There are plenty of women who are won by "unlikely" guys because he stepped up, pursued and *DID* the things necessary to win her heart. Many guys may have liked this particular woman (I'm thinking of two specifically right now), but how many stepped up and asked her out? How many dared to believe they had a chance with her? It's now the guy with the ring on his finger! "The race is not to the swift and the strong" (Ecclesiastes 9:11), "but to those who persevere" (Matthew 24:3).

Are you willing to step up, be honest and put in the work necessary to get what you want? Or are you thinking it will just drop on you as you wait passively and do nothing different than you did before? I did this all through my thirties and it was a disaster for my dating life. I got what I "wanted," and what I confessed and believed—which was nothing. That shifted when I turned 40. You don't have to wait until then. You can change your thinking, and your confession and action, today!

SAYING 'YES' TO THE INSTITUTION OF MARRIAGE

You're not just marrying the person; you're marrying the institution of marriage. There are perils and follies, advantages and benefits, ups and downs to married life. It's not all kisses and roses (although those things are nice). You will have trials with whomever you marry. The question is, will you do better in those trials with this person, even if they helped cause some of them, or are you better off alone?

Why are so few older singles coming out of places like India, for instance? Because they're still doing it the traditional way. And there's no excuse because the system is set up to help produce those results.

Sometimes as evangelicals, we are so open-minded we let our brains fall out. Sometimes we're so open to the move of the Spirit that we accept the strange and even the unbiblical. We accept the lie that people are actually happier living in a single state than married, despite the Bible presenting scant evidence of this. Yes, Paul had a particular grace, but he's few and far between (most of the apostles had wives, for instance).

I think it's really about Christians not thinking God likes them. Not trusting their Father loves them and wants to bless them and give them the desires of their hearts. It's an orphan spirit, at the end of the day.

113

Worldly people don't have such baggage. It's black and white. I'm speaking in generalities here, but it's important to see that your attitude and beliefs have a huge impact on where you're at as well as which system you buy into. God opposes the proud but blesses the humble (James 4:6). Have you humbled yourself before Him, submitting not only your desire but your very being, laying down everything and asking Him to be Lord of *all*, including your desire to be married? Or are your prayers basically asking God to build your kingdom, do it your way and on your terms so that you don't have to face pain or the issues you're denying, hiding, and running from?

That's not the way of the cross, which daily crucifies the flesh and conforms it to the image of Christ, who laid down His life completely only to take it up again. He arose empowered and triumphant over death. Jesus wasn't triumphant over death when He healed the sick, multiplied food, and walked on water (although these were signs that He would be). He was triumphant over death when He went to the cross, entered the grave, and on the third day rose again.

Most of us want to walk in power, blessing, and have a vibrant spiritual life but are afraid to suffer. We'll do anything but deny ourselves and submit fully to our Father's will, trusting in His resurrection power to raise us up.

Jesus said if you seek to save your life in this world (hold onto, control, own), you'll lose it, but if you lose your life for his sake and the gospel (lay down, surrender, die), you'll find it (Mark 8:35). The only way in is to experience the cross. Have you embraced it in this area?

It doesn't mean lose your desires or your personality, but in God's refining flames and the death and rebirth process He will conform all things according to His plan. Do we trust our Heavenly Father and desire His Kingdom to come and His will to be done, on earth as it is in heaven, or do we still desire our own kingdom?

I lived in a fantasy world for a long time, believing it was normal. I always knew singleness wasn't the long-term life for me, but I couldn't bring myself to change my attitudes or behaviors, which would require facing my fears and getting over myself. I couldn't get off the throne of my life. I couldn't get out of my own way and let nature be nature (don't be so scared; God created our nature and wants to redeem it, including our desire for intimacy and connection).

I knew singleness wasn't for me because I kept desiring marriage. I would recoil when I saw most older single people, saying to myself that I didn't want to end up like them, single and alone later in life. I'm not saying they're all unhappy, but I knew this wasn't the life for me.

Yet even knowing that, I couldn't bring myself to change my behavior, to engage differently with God, myself, and members of the opposite sex and begin to see different results. Have you ever found yourself in this last predicament? Maybe this is your wake up call, your Kairos moment!

Maybe it's time to plot a new course, to shake off the old and get started with the new. There are better things ahead!

Chapter 10

DESPERATION

How Desperate Are You? My wife cried out to the Lord, fasted, and prayed for a spouse (after repenting of her past relationships), and her request was soon met. She asked some single friends to fast with her for the same thing. Their responses were that they weren't interested or that it was "sinful" or "fleshly" to pray for a spouse.

My wife's response? "I still want a husband and I'm going to fast anyway." Within a few months, we got married. Several years later, most of those friends are still single.

I realize many of you have prayed, and even fasted (although if you haven't tried that, I highly recommend it; see Resources for Fasting in the Appendix), and have not gotten married. That's what a lot of this book is about: breaking mindsets and shattering lies, in ourselves and in the culture, that keep us from finding marriage.

Clearly, they're out there, with a rise in perpetual singleness and a decline in marriage. Is this God's will or another sign of how our society has been turning from Him? And sadly, the church doesn't look much different. Yes, the marriage rate is higher, slightly, but so is the divorce rate (and don't let anyone tell you that it's 50 percent. That is a complete lie from the pit of hell trying to normalize divorce. See Appendix B for an explanation). Marriage is under assault, especially godly marriage. If we're not prepared to go counter-cultural then we can easily get swept up into the prevailing culture. We'll soon end up in a place we never intended.

Have you ever stopped and asked yourself how you got to where you are today? Have you ever looked back, not just at the relationships that didn't work but at the decisions you made to pursue or not pursue relationships, to wall yourself off or to be more public, to pray, to serve or to stay in business? Have you brutally assessed the factors that might be keeping you in the place you're at instead of simply blaming God or blaming other people?

And, like I said above, sometimes it's a cultural narrative that's killing us, pressures from family, coworkers, or the movies and TV we consume telling us to live a certain way or causing us to hunger for certain things that aren't biblical, aren't godly, and have nothing to do with the kingdom. We have to ask ourselves the hard questions before we can move forward because Jesus said, "you shall know the truth and the truth will set you free" (John 8:32).

Stop right now and think about things. How fulfilled are you as a single? How happy are you? On a scale of 1-10, how does being single stack up with your life goals? Will it allow you to fulfill your dreams? Is this something you want to continue? Look ten years down the line. Do you rejoice at the thought of being single in your forties?

If not, then let this be a point of reckoning and deciding how you want your life to look, how it got this way, and what you can do about it.

SOME COMMON DYSFUNCTIONS THAT I SEE

1. *Wanting a man, but not marriage.*

Some women have a lot of mistrust. They keep a man at arm's length because of past wounding and/or a father wound. They seek the approval of a man, sometimes by seduction, but don't trust him enough to marry him or entrust themselves to him. They want it both ways, to be the center of attention but also to be strongly independent. These are often from control issues based in fear. Remember that self-protection is sin and God won't glorify desires that are based in unrighteousness. The cross offers a better way—laying down our lives and letting God raise us up. This is the only way to get free from pride.

2. *Wanting marriage, but not a man.*

I've seen some women that greatly desire marriage but struggle to believe they're worthy of it, pretty enough, or even that they are desirable to a man. This actually makes it harder to find your mate, since confidence is a large part of what makes us attractive. Did you grow up with an absent dad or one that never affirmed your beauty? Know that your heavenly Father doesn't feel this way about you and He wants you to start agreeing with Him, not the lies of culture, the devil, or our family of origin. Seek counseling, inner healing or whatever it takes to banish these lies and start walking in the truth.

Sometimes this lack of confidence also affects your relationship with God. Are you praying in faith and do you really believe God's good, or do you secretly think He doesn't like you or won't answer your prayers? This is way more toxic than not having a husband!

There can be practical steps to make yourself look and feel more attractive, but outward beauty can't compensate for a woman that feels ugly on the inside. Conversely, a woman that doesn't have supermodel looks but knows who she is and is comfortable in her own skin is way more likely to find a mate than someone who's trying to be who they aren't.

3. *Want marriage, but not a woman.*

For men who say they want marriage but are too lazy to pursue a woman, they are often masking low self-esteem. Men hide in distraction, busyness, partying, or work to avoid feeling their ache for relationships—but it won't go away. Even lots of serving in ministry can't fill the void. Face what's holding you back. Contend for your own wholeness so that you'll have something to share with your wife (and be willing to take the steps to find one). Many guys I've talked to went through intense seasons of wrestling and working through their issues before finally finding contentment—and shortly after, their spouses! No pain, no gain. Face your issues, believing that there's breakthrough on the other side. It's worth it!

4. *Wanting a woman, but not marriage*

These are boys in men's bodies, wanting the joy of a woman but unable to commit and form a family. It can be control issues, a refusal to be vulnerable, and often results from past wounds or issues from the family of origin. If you're walking in this false bravado, it's actually a form of pride. Men like this have an inability to meet a woman's needs (which include security and commitment) and are ultimately self-centered.

This was me for years. I would be the hero or the star, but I was scared of someone seeing into me. I would work hard, perform, serve and impress but I couldn't humble myself and open up or trust that someone would like me for who I was (and as I was). So, I was on this rampant and wrong search for someone, or something, that doesn't exist—or is only found in Jesus — a love that will never fail.

Instead of hitting wall after wall, and breaking hearts along the way, why not humble yourself and repent? God opposes the proud but gives grace to the humble (James 4:6).

RUNNING & HIDING

Both sexes can withdraw from the fight. Some women become really mousy or girlish because they don't want to be taken seriously. Others choose to not look good or even dress boyish in order to not attract attention. It's almost like they're daring guys to be attracted to them or notice them, because they're pretty sure they won't. Their solution is hoping to be ignored rather than facing their frustration and disappointment. Yet the desire won't go away, and it's there for the taking if you overcome your fears. The antidote to fear is faith.

Some guys (and girls) check out through busyness, works or serving. Through rampant effort, drive and motivation, we build walls around ourselves to create a zone where we feel safe. This is a normal response to sin; we hide and cover, just like our first parents in the Garden. But we can also choose to stop doing this! We can change our mindsets, come out of unbelief, and step into faith. This is called repentance, and it leads to life!

If God is giving you the gift of singleness, even for a season, there will be grace for it. Where God guides, He provides. But don't mistake a season for a lifetime! Sometimes we get so comfortable in that season, and the benefits it provides, that we assume things will always be this way. But that's not God's plan and He will come and prune us "so that we may bear much fruit."

God always wants more fruit. He wants us to increase and multiply. Do we believe this? You could even start praying, "God, thank you for helping me increase and multiply." Now we recognize there are seasons for this to happen, an appointed time and place. It won't always be instant and we can't control times and seasons, but praying this way puts you in agreement with God's agenda for our lives and starts us on the journey of receiving His best.

Prayer:

"Lord, thank You for helping me increase and multiply (it's a command, not something we passively await but something we do). Show me how to partner with You in this, including what steps to take, even if that step is waiting on You at this time. Thank You that You are good and I'm called to reflect Your glory. Thank You for helping me, in Jesus' name."

And when you find someone:
1. Get in touch with your feelings.
2. Ask good questions.
3. Walk out the necessary steps.

THE PRAYER THAT
BROUGHT ME MY WIFE

Something I didn't share is how I had prayed to meet my wife during the overnight shift at the prayer ministry where I serve (Our prayer room is staffed 24 hours a day, so people take shifts throughout the day and night to keep the live prayer and worship going; you can see it live at IHOPKC.org or search 'IHOPKC' on YouTube).

I was on the night shift for a year and a half and didn't meet anyone. Five years later I joined the night shift again and, boom, met my wife. I never got bitter when it didn't happen the first time. I simply concluded God had other purposes or plans for me during that time (He did; I needed to be focused on my studies), that I wasn't ready yet (I wasn't, emotionally or in life), or that my

126

wife wasn't ready yet (she lived thousands of miles away until shortly before we met).

I don't believe there's only one person we can marry in life, but I do believe God knows whom we're going to marry and is guiding us toward that person, if we stay open. I put my faith in His character and the process, not what I could see with my own eyes (which looked pretty barren). I partnered in prayer, praying this specific prayer I'm about to share when I had no evidence it was working. In due time, I reaped a great result!

Positive thinking, and positive speech, when it aligns with the Bible, is powerful! That's why I am a fan of making a *positive* confession as you pray. The prayer that brought me my wife was based in one key phrase. Can you guess it? It's not "Please," or, "Lord would you ..." (I'm always a little amazed when Christians pray, "Lord, would you just ..." I'm not here to beg God). We all have our moments of desperation where we simply cry out, but praying over a sustained time requires praying in faith. Here is the prayer that I made on a near daily basis (sometimes multiple times per day):

"Lord, thank You for the beautiful, amazing,
godly woman that you have for me to marry.
Thank You for leading me to her and her to me,
and thank You for preparing me for her and her
for me."

Do you notice the first word of each line of the
prayer? It starts with *thank you*. I started out by
thanking God for the wonderful and amazing
spouse he had for me, not asking Him for it. Why
did I do this? It's because I believed that it was
already done. If you're in your thirties, there is
almost a 100% chance that your spouse is alive
right now. Therefore, you're praying for a real
person who is alive at this time. You can pray for
God to prepare them and guide them, and you
can thank God for the person they are and are
becoming, how they will be compatible with you
and be a good fit, bringing you closer to the Lord.

It's amazing when I pull back the veil and see
how God honored that prayer over the *years* that
I prayed it, long before I ever met my wife. I see
now how He was in fact guiding her, leading her
and preparing her so that when we met we were
ready for each other. We didn't instantly fall in

love, but we were ready to become friends over a six-month period, and then when God opened my eyes, I was ready to pursue her.

I prayed this prayer years before Stephany ever moved to my city, and even before she was in the United States (my wife is from Ecuador). And I was praying that prayer during the season when she moved to Kansas City expecting to stay for only two weeks, and then God told her not to leave. He kept her there for nine more months until we met, and then, during another season shortly after when she could've left again. This was all before we had begun our romance. God was so faithful and honored my persistent prayers. Of course, it took longer than I would've thought and I had no way of knowing *how* it would be fulfilled (or with whom), but the beauty of this prayer is it gives God an open door of faith, which is the primary thing He's looking for ("For without faith it is *impossible* to please God," Hebrews 11:6 says; emphasis added).

I didn't make specific physical recommendations or requirements of what I wanted, but I did tell God it would be someone I was attracted to, someone who is amazing, someone who is an asset and a joy to be with and many other things. **The beauty of this prayer is it combats so many of the lies that we believe.** Most of us are struggling on some level to believe God has someone who is great, godly, attractive and any other number of good things. Our fear is that God doesn't really love us or He's going to make us settle or pick someone who is mediocre just so we can end our singleness. This is *not* God's heart. I know that's hard to believe the longer that you stay single, but this prayer really helped me combat the lies and assaults that I faced from myself, the devil and sometimes from others.

The power of life and death is in the tongue and I've long believed in making positive declarations. You may be saying, "What if God doesn't have someone super attractive for me to marry or doesn't give me all of the things that I request?" I would say pray according to your faith. I also believe that if God picked someone who's not physically attractive at first sight you can grow into finding them attractive. God's goal for you in marriage is not to grit your teeth and bare it, but to develop love and attraction to the person.

In those rare cases where you don't feel much physical attraction, if it really is the person God has for you then I believe He will give you confirmation and grace to move forward. (The Bible also says that physical beauty is fleeting). Again, these situations are rare and in almost all marriages there is a good level of attraction between the pair, which is one reason they decide to get married. I'd rather come in faith and believe for someone I'm attracted to, or some other important qualities, than believe for almost nothing and get even less.

Another reason to pray this prayer is it's biblical. The Bible says to make your requests *with thanksgiving* and, believing that you have received it, it will be yours (Philippians 4:6 and Mark 11:24). Let's get washed in the water of the word right now and renew our minds:

"Be anxious for nothing but in *everything* by prayer and supplication, *with thanksgiving*, let your request be made known to God, and the peace of God, which surpasses all understanding, will guard your hearts and minds through Christ Jesus (Philippians 4:6-7, emphasis added).

"Therefore I tell you, whatever you ask in prayer, *believe* that you have received it, and it will be yours" (Jesus in Mark 11:24, emphasis added).

Paul doesn't say just pray and berate heaven with your requests; he exhorts us to include thanksgiving. *When's the last time you prayed with thanksgiving for your future spouse?* When's the last time you thanked the Lord for their existence and their current state, or even their good attributes? Do you know there's many things that you want, certain things you're attracted to, certain spiritual traits, whatever it is. Why not ask the Lord for those things or, better yet, start *thanking* Him for them? If you truly believe that He can or will give them to you then why not start thanking Him?

It's like if a parent tells a child they're going to get them a new bike in a few months, maybe for Christmas or their birthday. The child naturally believes it's going to be a good bike, something they will like and enjoy. They're probably going to get excited, start talking about the gift long before it is received and be happy during the time of anticipation. They may have moments of frustration in the waiting—most people don't like to wait—but they would have an overwhelming confidence in the goodness of their parents, and the goodness of the coming gift, that would shield them from becoming bitter or refusing the gift before it is delivered. If a child can be believing, and grateful, before the gift manifests, how much more can we do this with our heavenly Father, who is the giver of "every good and perfect gift" (James 1:17)?

I don't think it's presumptuous or out of line with faith to do this. In fact, I think an unwillingness to do this shows, or can show, a lack of faith, an orphan or a beggar mindset. If we're saying things like, "I don't want to be prideful," or "I don't want to demand too much," we're actually saying that we don't believe God will give us much, that He doesn't really love us or care about us. These are frequent accusations, and not only from singles, although being in your thirties and single can help those tendencies to mount up. Overcome them and combat them directly with a spirit of thanksgiving when you pray. That's why the prayer I'm suggesting is a good way. It's a knockout punch.

When I was working as a journalist, we were supposed to say things as concisely as possible and not be wordy, so I really enjoy this prayer because it knocks out two birds with one stone. It's both intercession *and* thanksgiving, or supplication and thanksgiving, and it fits right in line with what Paul exhorts us to do.

What will be the fruit if we pray this way? According to Philippians 4:7 the peace of God will guard our hearts and minds in Christ Jesus. Do you want that peace? Even as a single person, even in your thirties, even with no prospects in sight? It's not really faith if you can see it. "Blessed are those who have not seen and yet believe" (John 20:29). Activate your faith today and begin thanking God for the amazing, wonderful, godly, compatible spouse that He has for you! Again, I'd rather ask Him for a lot and get a little than ask for a little and get even less (thank you Mike Bickle for teaching me this). History goes to the believers, not the doubters. Stop being down on yourself and down on God. He wants to bless you. Partner with Him to see it manifest.

I'd also like to note that when you pray this prayer, you are giving up control. By acknowledging that God has a plan, that He has someone amazing for you and that He's actively working to prepare and guide you to them (and them to you), you're putting your faith in the process and in the character of God, not in a specific result. And by specific result I mean the timing or details, like the way He's going to do it, or even who exactly with. This is surrender and honors God because you're upholding His good character and His good heart for you and not trying to box Him in. He likes it when we move in faith.

Epilogue:

You Can't Steer a Parked Car

The hardest car to steer is one that's not moving. With even a little motion, however, when you turn the wheel, you almost instantly begin to see change.

Stop hiding in holy inaction, which quickly leads to dissatisfaction. Yes, there is a place for holy waiting, but quit using your waiting as a disguise for unbelief. There are many of us stuck in inaction when we're truly dwelling in unbelief. That again is a difference with the world. They don't have a place for that. They simply go for what they want and, if they don't, they have a good reason for it. There's no waiting, disbelieving or being stuck, and even better, there's no religious language to couch it in or groups of people around them that will condone their passivity!

Again, I'm all for prayer and godly waiting upon the Lord, but even what it means to wait in faith is different from how it may have been taught to you. "Faith without works is dead," James 2:26 says, and waiting in faith includes faith-filled action as you wait. Yes, we're not called to wait frantically, but action applies both spiritually and naturally. Consider these things as you pray and talk them over with your pastor and spiritual counselors.

"The more Jesus you have, the more clarity you'll have," a friend of mine says. The clearer you are, the more righteously desperate, the more humble and surrendered to God you are, the more quickly He can work in your life. That's my conviction, based on my experience and what I'm sharing with you. And if you think you excel at these things but aren't seeing fruit, it's worth asking if you have blind spots or areas of your life you haven't surrendered. Sometimes we're using a religious box to hide our insecurities.

For men, change your actions; for women, change your attitude. Not that it's exclusively one or the other—many people need to work on both —but predominantly for men it's start acting differently, and very often for women it's change your mindset. Now for men to change their actions they sometimes also have to change their mindset. But more often than not it's a question of putting into practice what they say they believe, or what they do in fact believe but just aren't doing. This can be called spiritual alignment.

The Lord wants health and wholeness and He will give it to all who genuinely pursue Him. But it's a no-holds-barred pursuit where He is touching every area of your life and nothing is off-limits. Too many of us have limited Him to our prayer or religious life but won't let Him touch our dating and romantic life, or even admit that we want it. But Jesus is Lord of *all* and wants to be acknowledged as such. He is trustworthy and good and wants to give you the very best. Come into alignment with Him today. I'm excited to see the results!

Appendix A:

WHY THE DIVORCE RATE ISN'T

50 PERCENT

This myth came into being in the 1970s when the number of divorces hit half the number of marriages in a given year. In other words, if there were 2 million marriages and 1 million divorces in one year, the divorce rate was 50 percent, right? That sounded good but there's something glaring that was overlooked: what about all of the *existing marriages* that *didn't* break up that year? Once that's factored in, the statistic changes entirely. Let me explain.

If the number of existing marriages in the U.S. is 50 million and you add two million marriages in a year, you have 52 million marriages. If one million of those broke up that same year, then the divorce rate looks like 1 out of 52, or about 20 percent (the statistics I've seen put it between 20 and 30 percent, with more educated women scoring on the lower end of that spectrum).

What also needs to be considered is that the number of first marriages that break up is much lower than second, third (and fourth) marriages. Researchers have found if you have more than one divorce, you're more likely to have multiple more. The divorce rate among first marriages is actually quite small, but people who routinely get divorced drive up the numbers.

This confirms that most of us are looking for happiness and contentment in marriage, and most people find a way to make it work. We also know people who, after one divorce, stay single or remarry to someone better and stay with that person. The desire for consistency remains and we're not made to "go it alone" or to go from partner to partner, no matter what our secular culture tells us.

Sadly, the lie of the "50 percent divorce rate" has gone largely unchecked in the media and the Church so Christians are susceptible to the same plague as the world. Let's start bucking the trend! Stop confessing the lie and start proclaiming the truth. God designed marriage to be good and lasting. Let's reassure one another that this is still His plan!

For further reading on this topic, I recommend *The Myth of the High Rate of Divorce* by Kalman Heller, available on PsychCentral.com.[1]

_____

[1] https://psychcentral.com/lib/the-myth-of-the-high-rate-of-divorce#1 Accessed March 2023

Appendix B:

RESOURCES FOR FASTING

Fasting marked a significant portion of my 30s. It's an excellent activity to do when you're single because it can help you draw closer to the Lord and also learn more about yourself. Instead of lamenting that you are eating alone, take that time to feast on God. You will be a safer, and hopefully more mature, person when you do meet your spouse if you've experienced clinging to Jesus more than anything, including food and the comforts of this world.

It's also easier to fast as a single because you don't have a spouse hoping to have dinner with you every night ☺. Take this time to focus on the Lord—He wants to be your first love, now and always!

These articles on fasting can help you get started and learn how to make fasting a regular part of your lifestyle. There are many good resources on fasting, but these are a great place to start. Happy reading (and fasting)!

(Disclaimer: This is not medical advice. Please consult your health professional if you have health concerns before doing any fasting.)

You can find these articles on IHOPKC's blog at www.ihopkc.org/resources/blog/

1. **The Why and How of Fasting**

2. **Tips for Fasting**

3. **How to Overcome Challenges in Fasting**

4. **Straight Talk About Fasting**

5. **The Wisdom of Fasting Weekly**

Adam Wittenberg is a writer, evangelist, and intercessor committed to proclaiming the truth about Jesus to as many people as possible. He formerly worked as a journalist, and now spends his time interceding for revival, communicating God's Word, and telling people about Jesus. When not writing books, you can usually find him spending time with his wife, Stephany, teaching middle school, or attempting a game of volleyball.

He can also be found on YouTube as The Bearded Prophet.

To inquire about one-on-one or group coaching, visit:

singleinyour30s.com

Made in the USA
Coppell, TX
27 April 2023